M000250587

LANDSCAPE TRANSFORMED

LANDSCAPE TRANSFORMED

AD ACADEMY EDITIONS

ACKNOWLEDGEMENTS

Cover: Background, landsat image of American corn belt, Northern Iowa (NASA); inset image, overview of Will Alsop's riverside scheme at Northampton.
Frontis: Garden of Fine Arts, Kyoto, Japan. (Courtesy of Tadao Ando, photograph by Shigeo Ogawa.)

Attempts have been made to locate sources of all photographs to obtain full reproduction rights, but in the very few instances where this process has failed to find the copyright holder, apologies are offered. All visual material is courtesy of the architects and authors unless otherwise stated. Photographic credits: Edward Blake, pp63 (centre and right), 64 (centre left, below left), 65 (centre and below); Dixi Carrillo, pp71 (below), 72 (above right, centre right), 73 (above), 75, 77 (below); Martin Charles, pp6 (above), 101 (centre); Lynn Crosby Gammill, p62; JJ Photoservices, p101 (above and below); Fran Leadon (Balmori Associates), pp44 (above), 45; Alex S MacLean (Landslides), pp10 (below), 13 (above); Mitsuo Matsuoka, p22 (below); Satoshi Mishima, p22 (above); Hiko Mitani, p77 (above and centre); David Walker, p76. Several images in this book have been published elsewhere, and in such cases, we would like to thank those who have given permission for their reproduction: p19 from Shigemori Mirei, NTSZK, vol 2b (Tokyo) 1938; pp30 (below), 33 courtesy Ordnance Survey; p34 from GA Jellicoe, *Studies in Landscape Design Volume II*, Oxford University Press, 1966; p35 from IRM McCallum (ed) *Physical Planning*, The Architectural Press (London) 1945; p37 (above and centre) from GA Jellicoe, *Studies in Landscape Design*, OUP, 1960; p37 (below) from GA Jellicoe, *Motopia: A Study in the Evolution of Urban Landscape*, Frederick A Praeger (New York) 1961. The aerial photograph of Wimpole, p41 (below), is Crown Copyright/MoD.

First published in 1996 by
ACADEMY EDITIONS
An imprint of

ACADEMY GROUP LTD
42 Leinster Gardens, London W2 3AN
Member of the VCH Publishing Group

ISBN 1 85490 452 3

Copyright © Academy Group Ltd. *All rights reserved.* The entire contents of this publication are copyright and cannot be reproduced in any manner whatsoever without written permission from the publishers.

Distributed to the trade in the United States of America by
NATIONAL BOOK NETWORK, INC
4720 Boston Way, Lanham, Maryland 20706

Printed and bound in Singapore

CONTENTS

LANDSCAPE TRANSFORMED
Michael Spens

This publication was inspired by the open-ended debate generated by an Academy symposium on the Recovery of Landscape, chaired by myself and Alan Balfour, which followed a one-day symposium at the Architectural Association. These two days, 17-18 March 1995, can be seen in retrospect to be the first major forum in Britain for new focus on the condition of modern landscape. As such, new ground was broken for England, where for too long we have been obsessed with historical landscape and the conservation of heritage at the expense of focusing on the condition of twenty-first-century landscapes, even while they are under way.

That said, it has to be recognised that these two days – which drew together a wide range of European and American talent, and numerous examples by way of presentation, of wholly new ways of perceiving landscape – were both inspirational and also inconclusive. What is therefore interesting is the degree to which the range of case studies which are published here have challenged old perceptions, and give good cause for confidence in the future exercise of landscape architecture. As the two-day symposia participants dispersed, that did not seem likely. Harder evidence had to be collected. As editors we have not included all the presentation material, seeing this publication not as a document of what has passed but as a continuation of a sequence of ideas. The valuable exposition by Dorothée Imbert on the evolution of twentieth-century garden design in America, and in particular the lecture by William Curtis will undoubtedly find full publication elsewhere: both contributions were notable.

The Recovery of Landscape, then, is a meaningless phrase, or else it can mean all things to all. Was landscape lost, like Arcadia, or Paradise in the works of Claude and Poussin, only to be recalled by set pieces of view-painting, or in the new stage sets of the heritage industry? I think not: James Corner, in his various presentations and interventions, on both days, demonstrates emphatically that it was never mislaid, did not need a recovery vehicle to tow it back across the spoil, and is polymorphous, vibrant with growth and change. It is rather the inhabit-ants of the twenty-first century zones of habitation, with our misreadings of obscenity, who grasp recovery as an option, recovery of consciousness, symbolism, spirituality, and if our consciences will allow, truth itself.

At the AA, Georges Descombes, Christophe Girot, Adrian Geuze and Jeffrey Kipnis all demonstrated that they had achieved full engagement in a new way with specific environments. Alan Balfour's own presentation, by contrast, gave us something of a pigeon's eye view of Berlin – that of a century-old pigeon, sombre and grey, ruffled and defiant; appropriately unimpressed by the devious machinations of the past decade; epitomised as six Landscapes of Memory, a Leipzigerplatz haunted by evacuation into amnesia. The curious reality of Berlin, as landscapists immediately realise on arriving there, is the abnegation of green landscape, notwithstanding the proliferation of valerian and other wild growth across the abandoned empty spaces. At the AA it was a relief, of a kind, to hear Marc Treib's civilised and hedonistic diatribe from California, where emphatically vegetation is not a kind of spatial building material. Treib was wise to warn that architects have a habit of adopting 'greenery' yet lack knowledge of its true 'material' qualities. Treib identified time as the crucial characteristic in landscape design, running in century-long cycles. Adrian Geuze drew us to recognise the anti-aesthetic standpoint, seeking radical means of applying such an awareness of change, to the landscaping of airports – bringing in clover seeds not roses, to draw in bees, so to propagate Dutch elms. Geuze showed himself to be already a veteran of the professional's tactical interplay with entrenched bureauc-racy. And memorably, in an Alpine landscape of century-old tourist aspirations, Georges Descombes revealed a new poetry, echoing in some ways the odysseys of Richard Long or of Hamish Fulton. In the wider world, landscape design is alive and well, even if embattled.

In James Corner's disappearing landscape was revealed the death of an artefact of silken lies, seductively enfolding the prostituted and overblown rural building blocks of a discrete Dupont estate, they too begging a heritage classification: perhaps those landscapes could one day also grow over such arcane buildings of sinister intent in a subliminal wave of abundant free growth, liberating the trapped ecologies from such presumptions of material well-being. From Corner sprang the vital cue of the whole event, the moment to go forward and embrace the future of the past, now and not tomorrow.

The Royal Academy seemed suddenly to be bursting with Poussins, to an altogether hyper-abundant extent; a 'feel-good factor' in contrast to the dismay and inconclu-siveness of late twentieth-century woes in the symposium. Poussin was nature's man, and was in this curatorial episode released from previous assumptions, 'bluntly' put, that is. It was perhaps the perfect conjunction of exhibi-tion and symposium, as the organisers had wisely fore-seen. The evening lectures in retrospect – the gallery darkened for slides against the foliage backdrop of the Poussin array – ranged from Peter Latz's remarkable reclaimed landscapes, to the wholly architectural language of Miralles. When the sound went off, and the lights came on, the dissonances of the afternoon symposium seemed evanescent, gone to grass. Peter Latz's hands were as dirty as Poussin's own, Latz with love for a lost world of industry now re-charged with poetry of place, even allegory (*see pages 54-61*).

William Curtis has recently turned his own historian's sights on landscape and attempted to define how a land-scape, as with architecture itself, or film, has a number of formal levels of meaning, grouped together and conn-ected at key points, yet also carrying allusions and wider strata of significant meaning. Ranging from the landscape of Castle Howard to the slopes of Java, landscape 'trans-forms tangible elements into the counters of a metaphysi-cal stratagem'. Curtis admits the necessity of language. By absorption or transformation, new 'maps' are made, such as are indicated by the landscapes of Claude Lorrain on the one hand, or Utzon's famous concept sketch for the

Sydney Opera House – clouds over sea, on the other – such are topographical abstractions.

The remainder of Curtis' lecture elaborated this point with a series of appropriate imagery from all periods, including the work of Richard Serra. But he was also careful to point out the usages common in man-made landscape: such as the language and growing technology of both agriculture and viniculture across the world. 'Making landscapes is about capturing space', he said, endorsing the importance of the urban edge, 'a non-place lacking civic or rural identity', and raising key questions:

- How to make a landscape, balancing the need for images of nature with the realities of high technology and rapidly transmitted information.
- How to create a space of democratic freedom which combines a social theatre with the appropriate privacy and contemplation.
- How to draw upon the lessons of history without regressing into pastiche or a superficial game of quotations.

Curtis referred to John Dixon Hunt's statement, 'Nature is not a stable objective norm against which art is assessed, but of course a kind of construct, something that we constantly have to redefine.' In other words, he identified the problem as being how, as always, to make authentic symbols, articulating a world view in which an ethical idea of nature has to be a major component.

He portrayed the landscape historian as exploring contemporary landscape constructs (as by Gaudi, Aalto, Asplund, Lewerentz, Scarpa, for example) to establish underlying common principles, for continuity and for transformation. Here, for Curtis, lies a world of mythical content of an equal richness to its historical equivalents. Such a condition offers 'portents of mythical space'. He recognises that human impositions on the landscape, such as railway lines, telecommunication systems, even traffic signs have the potential, within a generalised vernacular, for the release of creativity. He considered that:

The most cogent conceptions of landscape are rooted in the cosmologies embodying sublime world visions. Nature and agriculture are transformed by technology and new moral and political definitions of culture are invented. A new ideal of social and ecological harmony, free of dangerous determinisms is required, one which would still address the relationship between people, places, technologies, traditions and everchanging definitions of the natural. These could even be found in this symbolic, an updated version of Poussin's notion of the Ideal.

The previous debate during the afternoon sessions suffered perhaps from a general lack of precisely this degree of critical focus. In retrospect, the short slots permitted a range of invited speakers to give valuable if disconnected contributions to increase a general awareness of the dimension of the problems posed by the revision of landscape philosophy as the millennium looms.

Peter Cook's intervention referred to a concept still common in Europe, of landscape as territory, 'occupied' not by enemy but by buildings in a form of urbanised collage. Referring back to the famous Sponge images, which previewed the shift in landscape usage, Cook reiterated his belief in green growth, applied as absolutely continuous by definition, and emphasised his interest recently in 'materiality'. Green material could, over a period, make interesting schemes more significant than before, even when this might involve a degree of structural decay. The statement by Treib that 'vegetation was not a plaything' did not invalidate Cook's point, where growth represented a natural continuum rather than mere surface treatment. The implication was that nature eventually reoccupies the territory.

David Jacques, landscape historian, again struggled to condense into twenty minutes what could have constituted a one-hour lecture on Modernist Landscape Theory. He sought to summarise the characteristics of the 'millennial mind-set'; to construct a cohesive theory from the varied statements of Brenda Colvin, Sylvia Crowe, Frank Clark, Ian McHarg – Sir Geoffrey Jellicoe was strangely absent from this list – but Jacques freely admitted, after probing by Sir Philip Dowson, the President of the Royal Academy, that this construct was an impossible ambition. Jacques produced a remarkable *aide-mémoire* (*see opposite*) which compressed the vagaries (as he saw it) of modernist determinism on a single A4 sheet. He claimed that the philosophies of Karl Popper were an invaluable tool today in the opposition to mere consensus, and the expression of true individuality. Jacques asserted that ecology was now taking a leading position in the table of priorities. Landscape architects (as professionally epitomised by Jellicoe) seeking to uphold landscape design as a high art activity, were not, he claimed, valid today. Cultural geographers, as represented by Dennis Cosgrove for example, are themselves now profoundly influenced by aesthetic considerations. Jacques stressed the major need for a full involvement of all professionals in the landscape project, and the futility of professional detachment: there had to be a search for new strategies, including a revision of ethics, 'modernists', he claimed, 'were not too concerned with ethics'.

James Corner here expressed the view that much of Jacques' thesis was some 'twenty years old' in principle, involving still a prescriptive mind-set itself. Alan Balfour took the opportunity here to offer a lament for the total absence of the 'new' in landscape interests in England. Other presentations published in this volume strongly endorse that view, notably Ted Cullinan and Will Alsop. As James Corner pointed out earlier:

> I think that landscape is a project and something has stifled that project in the past however many decades and one could analyse why it has been stifled; perhaps our modest education or perhaps how we actually think about landscape psychology and the semantics associated with landscape, because for whatever reason something has stifled creativity.

In this publication, post-symposia, we have endeavoured to demonstrate, notwithstanding the degree of bewilderment that pervades the professional and public domains on the matter of landscape design and future circumstance, that the reasoned optimism of, for example, William Curtis is indeed reflected in a powerful array of current projects from designers across the world, and that a constructive revision of priorities and attitudes is already under way. Whether we consider the Dacca proposals of Anuradha Mathur or the Arizona Canal project of Paul Friedberg, or the Singapore Arts Center landscape design by Peter Walker, or the new Charlotte University Campus proposals by Ted Cullinan, this is indisputably true. However there are, inevitably, no grounds for complacency. There is no 'feel-good' factor in the consumerist jargon of the present British Prime Minister. It is a fragile, and highly vulnerable global project. Currently, in educational priorities, professional commissions, public cognisance, and media ratings, there is little evidence of the recovery of landscape. Despite major awareness of conservation necessities, as John Phibbs shows, England's reservoir of landscapes by its most famous eighteenth-century exponent, Lancelot 'Capability' Brown, is rapidly being eroded by golf courses, high-tech farming and urban growth. Conservation needs an eye to future social requirements in a living, constantly evolving, natural continuum. If this is freeze-dried and fenced off, we have failed dramatically. But the vision is here, and the talent is limitless. That, at least, the events of the symposium in March have demonstrated unreservedly.

Michael Spens is a practising architect, author and critic.

Comparison of the Mind-sets of Modernist Landscape Architects with that Approaching the Millennium (D Jacques)

Aspect of Mind-set	Modernism in Landscape	Landscape at the Millennium
truth	faith provides ultimate certainty	ultimate certainty requires changeable conviction
knowledge	reduce to simple truths	welcome complexity and interconnectedness
generation of ideas	the *Zeitgeist*, the ecological imperative, genius	personal responsibility, the intellect, refinement
society's wishes	consensus	pluralist
view of the future	historicist – inevitable evolution of society	uncertain – depends on events determined by ourselves
tools of public policy	designers given pride of place	fiscal and management measures
who judges treatment	the artist, the expert	an informed public, assisted by critics
their means to judge	natural and instantaneous [inherited responses]	cultural and cognitive [aesthetics, meaning, ethics]
environmental perception	passive receptivity to objective truth	action and sense of place, determined by values
what to judge	from [neo-Platonism]	validity w.r.t. values
what makes beauty	attributes: harmony, texture	the aesthetic experience
meaning	symbolic power in Jungian terms	historical significance promoting understanding
ethical status of treatment	irrelevant, as judgement in artistic terms	political/ecological correctness

THE OBSCENE (AMERICAN) LANDSCAPE

JAMES CORNER

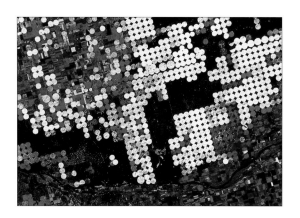

FROM ABOVE: NASA, landsat image of pivot irrigator fields over the Ogallala Aquifer, Garden City, Kansas; irrigation canal and fields in the desert, Bakersfield, California; OPPOSITE: NASA, landsat image of American corn belt, Northern Iowa

The term *landscape* generally brings to the minds of most people ideas of nature, beauty and scenery. At first, one might typically conjure up images of particularly benevolent scenes – gently meandering river meadows, rural farm fields, cottage cutting-gardens, or even the great aristocratic gardens of earlier periods. Less bucolic images may also be embraced, images of a Sublime and Picturesque nature: storms on the horizon, moving dramatically up the rugged mountain valley; great cavernous waterfalls and rivers in flood; gloomy forests with broken branches, fallen trunks and a sense of infinite dimension.

Although such images are not always of wholly natural features, gardens and rural fields are so easily equated with the larger natural landscape because their aesthetic, physical and temporal aspects closely resemble (and are caught within) the processes of the natural world. Thus, unlike buildings, landscape constructions tend to 'naturalise' themselves over time, masking their artifice and rendering invisible their underlying ideology.

Mention *landscape* to the average person on the street, then, and their first impressions will likely resemble the above in one way or another. Mention *landscape architecture* to the same person, and, if at first they respond a little puzzled – isn't landscape either natural (untouched), farmed (by farmers) or gardened (by homeowners)? – they will likely assume that perhaps the landscape architect is trained in the construction of scenery, in the composition of landscape elements so that a harmonious view will be presented. With more reflection, our innocent citizen may go on to conclude that landscape architects – in their work with roads, new built developments, tourist sites, forestry management, and so on – will make things appear to fit together, to put things in place, screening out the undesirable while preserving and framing the scenic moment. Even the most avant-garde of contemporary landscape architects, our average layperson may assume, is still likely to be preoccupied with scenic construction, albeit perhaps of an eccentric, seemingly abstract order. And here, of course, lie the contentious issues of taste and

style that have been intrinsically associated with landscape affairs since the seventeenth century, issues that remain embedded most deeply in local and regional conflicts between preservationists (heritage groups) and entrepreneurs (whether of economic, programmatic or artistic/creative impulse).

In this brief sketch, landscape remains an object of contemplation; it is presented (and conceived) as something to be beheld, typically from a distance. As such, landscape exists here largely as a visual image, a picture, albeit one that is dense with semantic value. Thus, many landscape architects have found a role to play in contemporary society that mirrors exactly what the above-imagined layperson would expect: they have emerged as scenic (and, increasingly, ecological) mediators, aiding in development while screening out (rendering invisible) its effects. Here, the site of landscape architectural work remains inscribed upon the all too precious scenic screen.

My own experiences of the American landscape have prompted me to be increasingly critical of the above view of landscape and landscape architectural work. For a variety of historical and cultural reasons, America presents a landscape that exceeds and challenges traditional notions of scene, garden and design. While these latter terms still have great currency in the United States – especially in the more 'European' eastern states – the larger landscape of the West remains less self-consciously shaped, presented less as a scene of contemplation or identity than an active and productive system. Granted, the great National Parks and wilderness areas are pervasively scenic and carry immense moralistic and semantic import with regard to the American imagination, but these are of relatively small and precious dimension compared to the hulking mass of the everyday, working landscape. Grids of interconnection, lines and arcs of pure circulation, endless circles and geometries of irrigation, cultivation and abandonment; dams, canals, mines, dumps, roads, tracks, transmission lines, strip-fields, silos, windmill fields, hydro-turbines, bomb test-sites, airfields, radio telescopes, levees, swales, woodlots, landfills, pilings, and plots of all possible dimensions and agendas. This is a landscape at work, an infrastructure of pure, inexorable presence. What one sees from the window of a continental flight are not merely curious patterns and forms but great metabolic scaffoldings of material transformation, transmission, production and invention. The entire country is an enormous working quarry, an operational network of exchange, movement and transmutation.

Consequently, I have come to appreciate the American landscape less as scenic space and more as one of time, network, event and production. Its closest European counterpart might be the Dutch polders, with their densely man-made landscape of pure productivity and presence. But the landscape of America exceeds that of The Netherlands: its immensity of scale is beyond comprehension, its effects are truly complex and dizzying, and its sheer explicitude is obscene, exhilaratingly obscene.

The transmutative, hybridising vibrancy of the working American landscape reflects the American dream. Always innovative, practical and efficient, the American mind is more preoccupied with action than with thought. Americans like to get things done, to be productive without reflection, without pretension. In turn, productivity is rewarded with material freedom, success and wealth. Sustained by the effervescent buzz of material accumulation, the American roams the land for opportunity. The instruments and results of such material utility are inscribed all across the land, ceaselessly producing, circulating, consuming, moving, hauling, draining, transforming. The lines and pathways of this active network have literally constructed a land of infinite accessibility, freedom and circulation. As much as this is often of a brutal and bland dimension, it is at the same time *effecting* of opportunity and availability.

With a brutal and unforgiving directness, then, the American landscape presents itself as the embodiment *par excellence* of industrial pragmatism, a pragmatism that is neither dull nor uninspired but spectacular in its banality, awesome in its creation of an idealised reality, or, to use Baudrillard's phrase, 'fascinating' in its 'actualisation of utopia', the consequences of which it must now (impossibly) evolve.

Thus, whereas America has an extraordinary share of truly remarkable natural scenes and designed parks and gardens, there is clearly another form of landscape at work here, one that is perhaps more propulsively diversifying in its effects and promise of a cultural Utopia than any scenic moment. To value or discredit this landscape from purely a visual perspective would be both easy and erroneous, for this is a landscape not of visuality but of furtive and busy inhabitation. It is not a landscape of space, enclosure and place (in the European sense), but a landscape of transiency, mobility, flux and change. It is the everyday landscape of every American, not the remote get-away, the gardenesque escape, or the scenic place of compensation that masks out all other ills. It is the site of both labour and dream, the real dream world of people manipulating, investing and living the land. Festering as much as it fosters, this landscape not only reflects the passages of time and life but also intimately instigates alternative passages and possibilities.

Appearances can be deceptive. The nostalgically inspired scenic screen alongside many modern roadways and developments often simply masks the inequity and the violence that lies beyond – industrial pollution, the play of capitalist real-estate markets, toxic land run-off, and other deleterious consequences of modern life. In a sense, this widespread tactic of landscape concealment is estranging in its effects, alienating the subject from its object, complicitous in the imperialist project. On the other hand, the brutal, massive structures that undergird the American landscape – while not always beautiful to look at, or 'virtuous' in connotation – embody a democracy at work, an ecstatic and obscene reality upon which inspired landscape architects of the future may find fertile sites for critical reflection and creative intervention.

To paraphrase Baudrillard, such landscapes no longer belong to the 'obscenity of the hidden, the repressed, the obscure, but [to] that of the visible, the all too visible, the more-visible-than-visible; it is the obscenity of that which no longer contains a secret and is entirely soluble in information and communication.' The ecstasy of such an obscene landscape lies in the elimination of the scenic gaze, of representation, and, instead, in the forging of a raw and self-presenting landscape, a purely indulgent and indulging medium of exchange, circulation, production, event and indetermination.

James Corner is Assistant Professor of Landscape Architecture at the University of Pennsylvania, Graduate School of Fine Arts. He has edited, together with Alan Balfour, a series of essays published in The Recovery of Landscape *from the Architectural Association.*

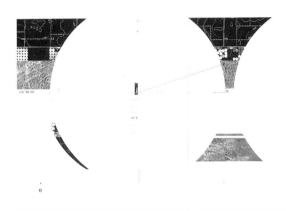

FROM ABOVE: Citrus groves with sprinkler irrigation, Blythe, California; pivot irrigator plot, Farmington, New Mexico, map notation

THE SOUNDSILENCE OF WATER

GÜNTER NITSCHKE

Furui ike ya	Old pond,
Kawazu tobikomu	Frog jumping,
Mizu no oto	Splash.

More must have been fantasised into and around this unique Haiku by Basho (1644-94) than into any other three-liner in world literature. But the poem does succeed to communicate to us why the sound of water has been so unconsciously attractive to humans of all cultures at all times. It can make us *hear* silence, and not only the silence after or between sounds, but the silence with and beyond all sound. We experience something of our own *original nature*, with and beyond all form and non-form. The sounds of a gunshot, a jet plane or a Harley-Davidson are hardly conducive to such 'experience'.

Somehow not satisfied with one occasional frog jumping into a pond, the Japanese gardener invented a mechanised version, a device to produce sounds of water splashing whenever he wanted it. Water from a garden stream was diverted and fed into the hollow end of a bamboo pole suspended on an axle at the centre; it would splash water back into the stream whenever the top end of the bamboo was full and top heavy. Empty of water, the bamboo falls back into its original position and hits a rock with its hollow end, producing the sound of shsh-plop at regular intervals that one encounters in many a Japanese garden. This device is popularly known as *shishi odoshi*, or 'deer scare', since it is reported to have been invented originally by farmers to scare off deer and wild boar. In reality it is closer to an ancient waterfall machine.

The tea masters of the fifteenth and sixteenth centuries, mostly lay adepts of Zen, were the ultimate artists in the use of water for its sound, form and haptic effects. Their intentions were naturally aesthetic ones, but often went beyond those – they did not only cater to the sensory delights of their visitors, but tried to sharpen their consciousness, too. Sen no Rikyu is quoted in the *Namporoku* to have stated, 'The tea ceremony of the small room is above all a matter of practising and realising the way in accord with the Buddha's teaching.'[1]

FROM LEFT TO RIGHT: Deer scare in the garden of Shisendo, Kyoto; tsukubai *in Katsura Detached Palace, Kyoto; dry cascade within the Saihoji Temple, Kyoto*

Many books have been devoted to the use, placement and form of *chosubachi* stones, the hand water basins initially placed in tea gardens in the sixteenth century, and later as merely decorative objects in almost all Japanese gardens, unconnected with the tea ceremony. In time they became works of art in their own right. In the tea garden the *chosubachi* was the largest in a whole group of carefully selected and arranged rocks, the whole composition being referred to as *tsukubai*, literally, 'a place where one has to bend down', that is, a place designed to rinse your mouth or wash your hands on the approach through the tea garden to the tea arbour. Sen no Rikyu comments on the meaning of water in the tea garden:

> In the tea garden, the host's first act is to bring water; the guest's first act is to use this water to rinse his hands. Herein lies the great foundation of the *roji* and the thatched hut. The stone basin is provided so that in the *roji*, the person who calls and the person called on together wash off the stains of worldly dust.[2]

The origin of this practice is religious; from approximately the thirteenth century on, such stones containing water for purposes of religious ablution can be found at entrances to Shinto shrines, Buddhist temples or cemeteries. Before that time, the Japanese went directly into the sea or rivers for ablution purposes.

Late in the Edo era these arrangements of rocks around the *tsukubai* reached the peak of their refinement in the so-called *suikin-kutsu*, literally, 'water-lute caverns'; you would hear a strange beautiful melody after dashing the water from your hands or mouth on to the pebbles spread around the *chosubachi*; where this melody came from would not be obvious. A large ceramic jug was buried upside down underneath the *tsukubai* and filled partly with water at the bottom. The reverberations of water drops falling three or four feet would penetrate through the hole at the top of the bell and then through the layer of pebbles on top of the jug to ultimately mystify the kneeling visitor.

Another famous poetic reference to the soundscape, rather than the landscape of a garden, we find in the *Hyakunin isshu*, 'Single Poems by a Hundred People', which dates back to the thirteenth century and is surely the most popular poetry anthology in Japan.

Taki no oto wa	Though the sound
Taete hisashiku	of the cascade
narinuredo	long since has ceased
na koso nagarete	we still hear the murmur
nao kikoe kere	of its name
	(Dainagon Kinto)

This poem supposedly sings of a well-known waterfall rock setting at the edge of Osawa Pond, where Emperor Saga (809-823) created a detached suburban palace for himself. What is even more amazing is that Shigemori Mirei, perhaps the most outstanding garden scholar of our time, believed that the waterfall contained no water; to him the excavated rock work of the cascade points to a dry waterfall.[3] Unfortunately, very little is left of the original setting which inspired the above poem. The oldest survivor and best-kept dry cascade can be found in the upper garden of Saihoji, the Temple of Western Fragrance in Kyoto. It is reported that in 1334 the Zen master Muso Kokushi took over the former Pure Land Buddhist establishment centring on a pond and spring garden for boating, and converted it into a Zen temple. As a counterpart to the existing pond and island scenery he created a *karesansui*, a dry mountain waterscape garden just where the garden borders on the mountain. This dry garden scenery came to function as something like a Mecca for future generations of Japanese garden designers; it is *the* prototype of *karesansui* as such, often mistakenly referred to as the Zen garden. In this garden the biggest attraction is a dry cascade where not a single drop of water splashes down the three-stepped, rather monumental rock work; still the roar of the water seems louder than at any other, even natural, waterfall in a Japanese garden.

The Cascade in Nature

The skill to construct waterfalls in gardens was obviously inspired by natural waterfalls abounding in Japan, a country with plenty of water. In Shinto, the Way of the Gods – an offspring of diverse local naturalistic folk beliefs of ancient Japan – is characterised by awe and worship of the unique in nature, such as strangely formed trees, rocks and mountains. Waterfalls were often venerated as *go-shintai*, or 'August Body of a Deity'. One of the best known natural waterfalls in Japan is the Kumano Nachi-san, which as *go-shintai* functions as the background for a dramatic fire festival held annually on 14 July.

From the Heian era onwards the original Shinto nature worship, practised in the beautiful environs of the Kumano River and the waterfall at Mount Nachi, became assimilated to Buddhist beliefs, especially those of the esoteric Tendai sects and Yamabushi mountain priests, centring around ascetic meditation practices deep in the mountains and the acquisition of magico-religious powers respectively. The Kumano Nachi Shrine Pilgrimage mandala from the sixteenth century is a vivid document and reminder of the syncretic nature of the Kumano cult, the central natural feature of which is the unique waterfall.

According to one school of Sino-Japanese etymology, the ancient pictogram for water is represented by an iconic sign of a waterfall with drops of water splashing right and left. The ideogram for waterfall itself shows a multiplication of the abridged iconic sign for water with that of dragon. There is a Chinese folklore tale pertaining to waterfalls and carps; the carp, with its scaly armour, was revered in ancient China because of its skill and perseverance to swim against currents and even climb waterfalls. Carps passing above the rapids through Dragon Gate are transformed into those most benevolent creatures of Chinese myth. This passage of the sturgeon became a metaphor for the excruciating examination hell that the Chinese had to pass through to be accepted into government service. Thus, many Japanese cascades feature a prominent rock with some semblance to a carp trying to scale the waterfall. The Dragon Gate Cascade, to the north of the Golden Pavilion in Kyoto, is not only one of the earliest existing but also most successful examples of a waterfall displaying in its centre a rock very close in form to a carp wriggling and trying to scale the cascade. This waterfall belongs to the few Kamakura era remnants within this estate in the northern mountains of Kyoto, whose name was symbolic of a whole era of Ashikaga culture during the fifteenth century.

Pond, river and cascade are the blood, rocks, the bones, and vegetation, the meat of the body of the Japanese garden throughout its many epochs. Naturally, each one of these three elements has undergone various transformations in history, a process which is far from complete. The latest transformation does not come from a gardener but an architect. It can be experienced in Tadao Ando's Garden of Fine Art in Kyoto, the building which inspired this essay (*see pages 22-23*).

The Cascade in the Garden

In the search for waterfall archetypes in Japanese gardens one does not only have to look at life models in natural nature but probably also to turn to the earliest records on garden making, such as the *saku-teiki*, the record on garden making of the eleventh century (see extract opposite). It contains a rather extensive section on waterfalls containing three items; technical remarks on the construction of rock formations for cascades, a typology of the most important waterfalls and remarks concerning some of their Buddhist symbolism.

The *saku-teiki* displays mainly a landscape feature-oriented approach to gardening; besides the above eight types of waterfalls, seventeen types of waterscapes or formations of islands and various ways of making garden streams are the main subject of this earliest record. Quite in contrast to that encyclopaedic quest for garden features, the next Japanese garden manual, dated 1466, *Senzui narabi ni yagyo no zu*, the illustrations for 'Designing Mountain, Water and Hillside Field Landscapes', by Zoen, indulges mostly in endless naming and description of rocks.[6] No detailed description of waterfall construction and compositions can be found in this manual.

No mention is made of dry cascades in the *saku-teiki*, even though the *karesansui* or dry mountain-waterscape garden is already described as a distinct type of garden although subordinate to, not independent of, the dominant prototype of garden existing at that time, 'the pond-spring garden to be savoured by boating'. The answer might simply lie in the fact that the dry landscape garden (with or without a dry cascade) became an independent, even dominating, prototype of garden only with the beginning of the Muromachi period in the fifteenth century.[7]

The question now is surely where these waterfalls of fancy, both with or without water, were located within the early classical gardens, and what they actually looked like. For documentation I shall choose two early, still well-preserved examples, one with water, the other without.

I

II

III

IV

EXTRACT FROM THE SAKU-TEIKI

Erecting a waterfall, first one should select a falling-water stone; that stone would not look interesting if it had a smooth front surface as if it was cut artificially. When the waterfall is made three or four feet high one should use a mountain rock with a slightly peculiar surface, which would render the waterfall more attractive. However, even though the water falls well and even though the surface of the falling-water stone is somewhat unique, all would be useless unless the support stones are set so as to harmonise with the falling-water stone and with each other . . .⁴

If the right side of the waterfall is to be formally emphasised, that is, the main aspect to be seen, then set a beautiful standing stone close behind the left support stone, and a slightly lower one behind the right support stone. If the left side of the waterfall is to be emphasised, then use the reverse order . . .⁵

In front of each of the right and left support stones one should place good side stones which are about half the size of support stones; and then set other stones following the demand of the former. It is particularly advisable to make the stream in front of the waterfall wide and place centre stones which divide the stream into right and left. The scenery further downstream should be that of an artificial garden stream . . . (see I, right)

If the water is made to fall from an unexpected slit within rocks, it adds to the mystery and depth of the waterfall. Therefore, one should place a fitting stone where the stream curves and shows its throat (A). *This makes the water appear, when seen from the distance, as if it comes out directly from the rocks . . .* (II)

There are various ways how water falls and thus different types of waterfalls:

here water is made to fall in equal manner facing each other in a beautiful way. (III)

if the water falls from the right (facing the waterfall), then a front stone should be set at the left side, which receives the water. It should be about half of the size of the falling-water stone; when the water hits the head of this stone, it will bounce off whitish and fall further down from the right now. (IV)

here the water is made to follow the creased and uneven surfaces of the rocks. (V and VI)

here the stone must have a sharp edge from where the water falls. One also has to let the water stream arrive rapidly without slowing it before the fall; then it will fall detaching itself from the surface. (VII)

here the front of the falling-water stone is turned slightly around and thus shows its side from the main viewpoint. (VIII)

first install a stone with a smooth surface as falling-water stone; the water before the fall should be stagnated and made to fall very leisurely; then the water will drop as if it was a sheet of cloth hanging. (IX)

set a stone with many jagged corners on its crest at the place the water is to drop; then the water splitting in many ways looks as if a large number of threads are hanging. (X)

first split the water into two courses and then, depending on the height of the waterfall, let the water drop in two or three steps without too much sophistication.

V

VI

VII

VIII

IX

X

The cascade in Tenryuji Temple in Kyoto together with its garden was designed as a Zen establishment by Muso Kokushi, who also created Saihoji. Without doubt, the wider rock formation of the cascade is the focus of the whole setting. The garden is composed to be viewed from the slightly elevated, fixed vantage point – the veranda of the abbot's quarters of the temple – framed by the eaves and the vertical posts of the porch. From there the garden presents itself in a manner quite similar to a Song dynasty landscape painting, in various consciously designed layers, even 'borrowing' the distant mountains to create depth. Zooming in on the opposite shore, the cascade appears behind a three-piece bridge over a narrow ravine; the rock group to the right in front of the bridge, echoing the Isles of the Blessed from Chinese myth, displays the most exquisite rock composition in the whole of Japanese garden history.

The new prototype of garden of the succeeding Muromachi epoch in the history of Japanese gardens was the *karesansui*. There are basically two variations, one presenting a completely abstract composition, as visible in the Ryoanji rock garden; the other a landscape painting type of composition in which most elements are often further overlaid with symbolism intrinsic to the Zen view of life and the world. The best existing examples of the latter are the various small courtyard gardens surrounding the abbot's quarters of Daisen-in, the Great Hermit Temple in Kyoto.

In the north-eastern corner of the premises one faces several rocks placed in a cascade formation over which the river of life, here painted with small white pebbles, starts and then plunges powerfully and joyfully over various rocks to form the mighty torrent of early youth.

It might be very surprising to a Westerner that a garden connoisseur like Shigemori Mirei states that – among the 1,025 historical gardens worth mentioning which have survived to our days – two thirds are compositions with real water in ponds and streams, and up to one third is dry.

The Cascade in Architecture

With 'Fallingwater' designed by Frank Lloyd Wright in the mid-1930s, the waterfall probably made its unsurpassable debut into modern architecture itself. Here the waterfall became an integral part of the architecture of a dwelling rather than just a feature in a garden attached to a dwelling. From that time on, cascades of any size, made of natural materials or plastic, as naturalistic or

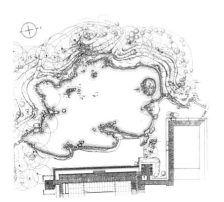

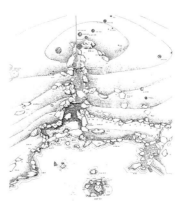

OPPOSITE, FROM ABOVE: Dry cascade in
the north-eastern corner of the court garden
in Daisen-in Temple, Kyoto; foyer garden in
ANA Hotel, Kyoto, with plastic waterfall;
isometric of dry cascade, Daisen-in Temple;
ABOVE: Cascade in Tenryuji Temple, Kyoto;
LEFT: Overall plan and detailed cascade
plan, Tenryuji Temple

completely abstract compositions, became important decorative features of the front or courtyards of large hotels, corporate headquarters, city halls, shopping malls and old people's homes all over the globe. A fundamental quantum leap in the concept of the waterfall was necessary to transcend the niceties of this endless series of ornamental falls of water that one had become used to in modern architecture.

Visiting the Garden of Fine Art in Kyoto from the Kitayama Road – sponsored by the Kyoto Prefectural Government and designed by Tadao Ando in 1994 – it is immediately obvious that this is neither a building nor a garden in the normal sense of the word. There are flowers, yes, but they are painted. The building really consists of a three-storey hole in the ground, reminding one to a certain extent of the famous deep-stepped wells in the Gujarat State of India. The Garden of Fine Art is an open-air museum exhibiting life-size replicas of famous works of art from both East and West in a kind of novel petrified ceramic form. As such they are made to last forever and withstand even the toughest weather; they will not corrode, fade or discolour.[8]

From the very beginning one is surrounded by ponds on both sides as one proceeds into the interior along a narrow concrete walkway. The first surprise is Monet's painting of *Water Lilies* – submersed in the waters of the pond, a very fitting and effective way of exhibiting this delicate painting. Proceeding further, it slowly becomes clear that this is a rather ambiguous world, part open-air museum, part space dominated by cascades. All the walls parallel to any movement are finished in raw concrete, all those at right angles to it are waterfalls. Cascades are faced frontally, an experience surely known to anyone; the visitor is made to quasi-enter them, descending with them from platform to platform, climbing up and down together within them. The visit is not only a spatial experience, but an olfactory and audial one, too; water-dust is carried about by the slightest breeze, as the visitor is totally immersed in the ever-present ambient sound of water.

At one phase the visitor may stand on a pointed promontory, looking down on to a scenery of man-made Niagara Falls surrounding Michelangelo's *Last Judgement*. Reservation may be expressed about the treatment of the 'flowers' of Western art, the religious art in particular. Admittedly, Ando's museum is no *Capella Sistina*; but our sacred places today might very well have shifted beyond churches. In addition, it ultimately doesn't matter what

art is exhibited here, European or Asian, sacred or profane; it clearly plays a secondary role to the art of space and place one is made to experience here over time. Like so many of Ando's buildings, this design presents a consciously created sequential experience of space with ever new and unexpected vistas; so the same painting is often viewed in different frames and settings. The most startling example is probably the sudden appearance of the three impressionist paintings by Seurat, Rouault and Van Gogh, standing free behind concrete windows which one suddenly faces when one turns the corner on the first lower level. Michelangelo's *Last Supper* has its own quiet spatial setting without any intrusions or extensions of any adjoining spaces; it is an oasis of its own.

One experiences spaces built of water, but no building. By digging a multi-level hole into the ground, the greenery of the botanical gardens is visually drawn into the scenery of the street. This contrasts with the parade of modern buildings designed as mere objects on Kitayama Dori, not as spaces, let alone places. They are mostly products of the Japanese economic bubble of the 1980s, when clients had so much money that they could afford to glue it on to the facades in the form of tons of twisted metal which then functioned as a metaphor for modern technology. These buildings no longer have any internal spaces worth entering or even mentioning; seen as objects only from outside, they already appear grotesque.

Paraphrasing my own remarks made on the character of traditional Shinto sacred artefacts, where I stated that deities can and do 'live' in objects, but human beings need spaces,[9] it could be argued that modern times contain bloated egos which enshrine themselves predominantly in and on objects; human beings mostly in spaces. Perhaps it is possible to read from their creations whether and when an architect has made the transition from an egomaniac into a human being who cares about others. After the creation of an anthropology of architecture, a need has arisen to lay a foundation for a psychology of architecture.

Objects, space and place have very different psychological connotations. Buildings as objects basically demand attention and admiration, buildings as spaces are invitations to enter, buildings as places are occasions to participate. Shin Takamatsu's Week 1986, Inning 1987 and Syntax 1994, close-by on Kitayama Dori, speak ultimately of one subject – the architect himself. In his buildings, wherever one looks or whatever one touches, the highly manneristic design or overdesign of Shin Takamatsu is evident; nowhere inside or around his buildings is there any relief, any escape from it. In this way, Takamatsu's buildings give you nothing; they just demand your attention, your energy.

It is really inadequate to call Ando's creations minimalist. They are minimal in the sense that they are not cluttered with all kinds of pieces of metal, as the buildings on the same street of his contemporary, Takamatsu, tend to be internally and externally. Ando's buildings are full of space, they are full of invitations and chances to enter, the walk around in, and just to be in.

It is tempting to infer that Ando's creations are Zen, or more exactly, are Zen in the sense of the seven salient characteristics which Shin-ichi Hisamatsu has distilled in his epoch-making seminal book on works of fine art, architecture and gardening influenced by Zen.[10] Here they are again: asymmetry, simplicity, austerity, naturalness, subtle profundity, detachment and tranquility. I would like to add another quality characteristic of Zen creations which one can discover in Ando's work: the hidden power to make you more conscious of yourself. Surely that must be art's ultimate endeavour.

In the case of Ando's Garden of Fine Art, the designer really has disappeared; he has been the legendary hollow bamboo on which creation played its tune, to use a Chinese metaphor. The visitor becomes immersed in the 'soundsilence' of water, the 'form-non-form' of space and the event/experience of place. The building abounds in conscious detailing: the handrails, for instance, ride on panes of glass; thus, visually there are no interruptions by way of vertical supports; a horizontal continuity is consciously set in contrast with the vertical rhythm of the falling water.

As water falls continuously over the edge of the ponds, the first ten or twenty centimetres of concrete wall appear to be absolutely dry behind the screen of water. Then the wall bends forward ever so slightly from the exact vertical to allow for a continuous splashing of the water downwards over the roughened surface of concrete. In the words of the *saku-teiki*, these must be the largest 'thread-like' falls ever created in the history of Japanese gardening.

Günter Nitschke works as an architect, urban planner and meditational therapist. At present he is Director of the private Institute for East Asian Architecture and Urbanism in Kyoto. He has taught at Princeton University and MIT.

Notes

1 Dennis Hirota, 'Memoranda of the Words of Rikyū – Namporoku Book 1', from *Chanoyu Quarterly*, No. 25, Urasenke Foundation (Kyoto) 1980, p33.

2 *Ibid*, p33.

3 In deep respect to my most important resource and mentor in the art of Japanese gardening, the late Shigemori Mirei, I here purposely reproduce some of the original measured drawings and photographs of the gardens of Saihoji, Tenryuji, Kinkakuii and Daisen-in, with as little change from my side as possible. Most later drawings of famous gardens are based on the unique life work of this garden scholar and designer, all of which were contained in *Nihon teien-shi zukan*, here abbreviated as NTSZK (Illustrated History of Japanese Gardens), 24 volumes, Yukuosha (Tokyo) 1936-89.

4 Günter Nitschke and F Nakazawa, *Saku-teiki – A Record of Garden Making*, unpublished, but well-circulated translation, 1968.

5 Katsuo Saito, *Zakai saku-teiki* (A Record of Garden Making: An Illustrated Explanation), Gihodo (Tokyo) 1966. His illustrations of waterfalls are reproduced here with kind permission of his son, Dr Kazuo Saito.

6 A complete translation of *Senzui narabi ni yagyo no zu* is contained in David Slawson, *Secret Teachings in the Art of Japanese Gardening*, Kodansha International (New York) 1987.

7 For a detailed exposition of the dry garden as the second great prototype in the history of Japanese gardening, see Günter Nitschke, *Japanese Gardens*, Benedikt Taschen Verlag (Koln) 1991, pp73-125.

8 Ceramic art is created from a positive photographic plate of a painting. The plate is transcribed on to a ceramic board which is then subjected to a calcination process. Many individual plates are joined together to form an original painting. The exhibited *Last Judgement* is constructed from 110 plates, 60cm by 3m in size.

9 'Daiiosai and Shikenensengu – First Fruits Twice Tasted', from Günter Nitschke, *From Shinto to Ando*, Academy Editions (London) 1993, p28.

10 Shin-ichi Hisamatsu, *Zen and the Fine Arts*, Kodansha International (Tokyo) 1971.

Garden of Fine Arts, Kyoto

Located next to a botanical garden on Kitayama Boulevard, this outdoor museum allows the visitor to enjoy masterpieces of Western and Japanese art while remaining in contact with the natural phenomena of light, wind and water. The museum reflects Tadao Ando's long interest in developing processional spaces along the approaches to projects such as the Water Temple and Church on the Water (both 1985-88). Here, such outdoor spatial sequences constitute the entire project.

An enclosed area is prepared below ground level within three walls, and circulation, consisting of bridges and ramps, creates a rich variety of spaces on three levels. Water is introduced into the experience through three waterfalls and pools at each level.

RIGHT: Looking north-east; BELOW: Lower floor, looking east towards Michelangelo's Last Judgement; *OPPOSITE, FROM ABOVE, L TO R: Perspective view from the entrance; paintings by Seurat, Renoir and Van Gogh framed by holes in the concrete wall; a 'window' in the eastern wall; plan; section*

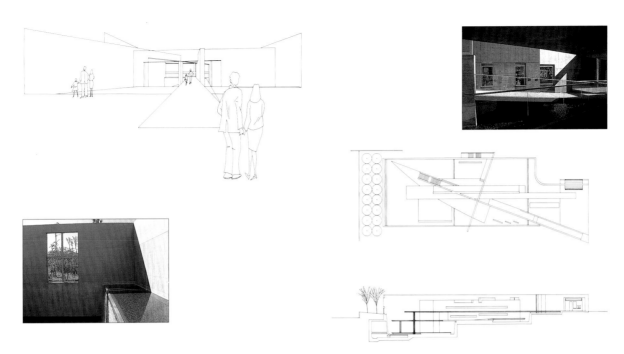

NEW LANDSCAPE AND GARDEN ARCHITECTURE
Hans Dieter Schaal

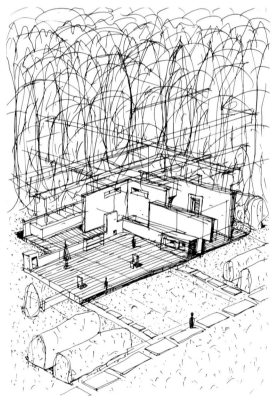

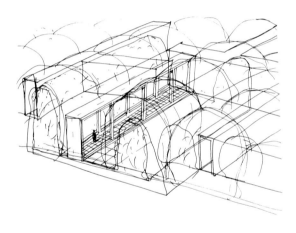

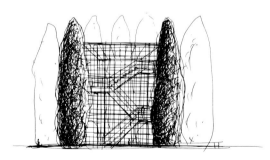

It is possible to use the brutality of architectural intervention in the landscape as a means of confrontation, but it can also be reduced by methods of adaptation and masking. One possibility of bringing the architectural body into connection with the landscape is interconnection. This process requires the architecture to dissolve into structures on the periphery of natural space that thrust into vegetation and are overgrown by it in the course of time

The tree as model: a branch structure is interwoven with space, bald and empty, then slowly covered over with buds, and finally covered with leaves

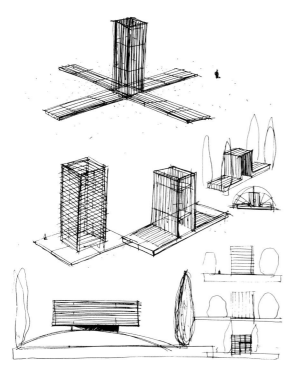

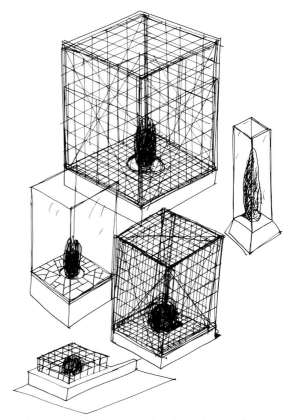

Space interconnection between showing and concealing

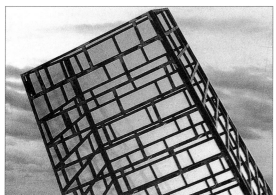

Buildings entirely dissolved into lines. Aerial framework. The wind blows through the architecture as if it were not there

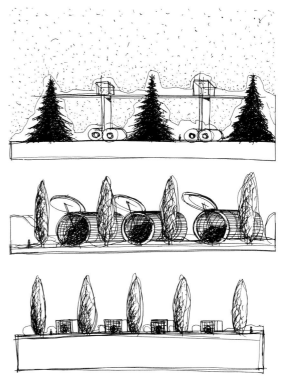

Vegetation attacks

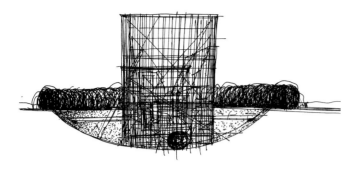

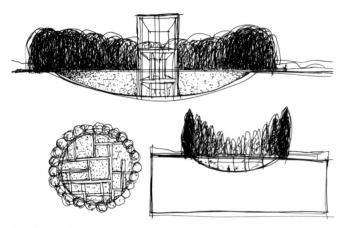

Slowly growing in. Summer image: the interconnection is complete. The artificial structure, the grid work, the line-architecture has grown in and become part of nature

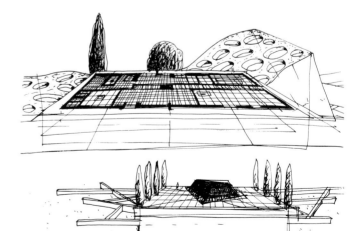

Ground plans for possible garden houses; ground plan garden

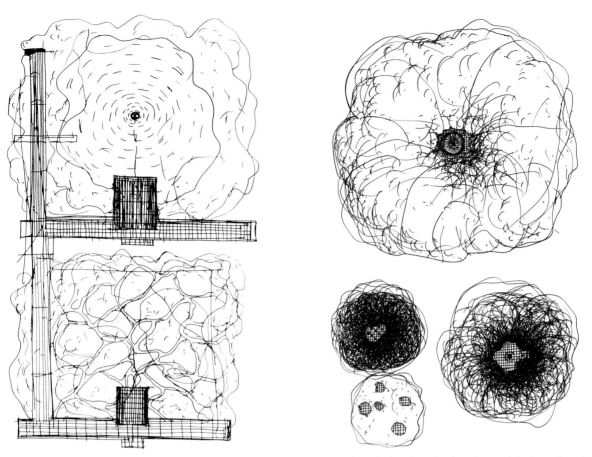

Imagine: you never go into the middle of the garden any more. A video camera installed at the edge broadcasts daily from the middle of the thicket, from nature's power centre.

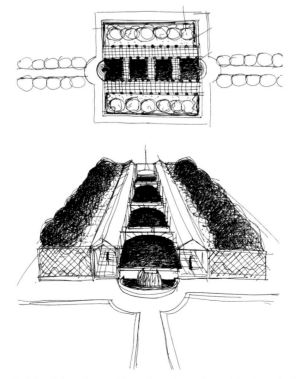

Residential gardens with pools and arcades, with arbour lattices, avenues, lawns, waterfalls, with bridges, ruins . . .

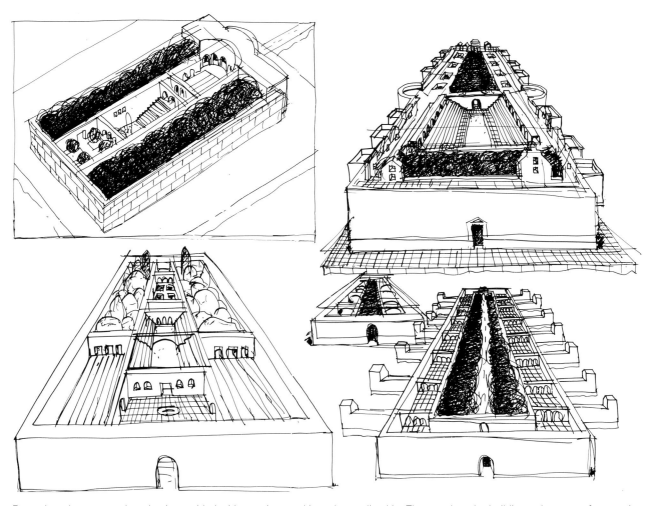

Extension: the courtyard garden is provided with openings and is no longer lived in. The arcades, the buildings, the rows of trees, the patches of lawn become a public garden; conceivable in the city centre as areas of quiet and as a substitute for church (secular monastery gardens). Or: the walled area is extended to form a settlement. A number of families live here. There are a central pool, steps, series of gateway-arches, arbours, groves, avenues, fields of flowers and accommodation. This area of interconnection opens up as well, the walls are no longer closed all round, the squares impinge on the city continuum or the landscape

Distant view: ways outward. The public garden, the new municipal park, garden programmes, garden stations, garden theme. Opened pictures. Possible to walk through. Public nature

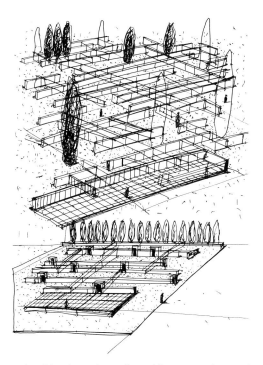

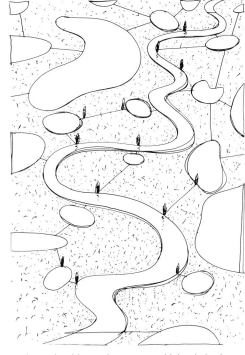

The gardens' borders, the walls and fences get lost and wander away in the open landscape. Large-scale movements increase

All interventions should remain traces and islands in the total 'landscape' continuum

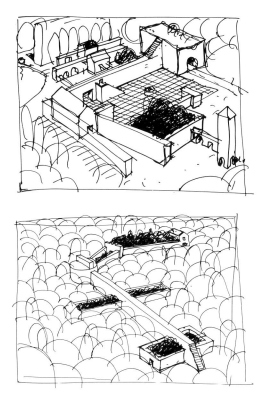

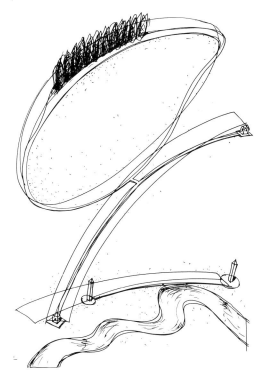

Paths with accompanying planting. Rhythms

Path tunes. Flowing. Restrictions, extensions. Edges of woods with buildings. Isolated towers. Culs-de-sac.

Hans Dieter Schaal studied architecture in Hamburg and Stuttgart, and since 1970 he has worked as a freelance artist, architect, exhibition designer, stage designer and landscape architect. This is an extract from his book Landscape as Inspiration, *Academy Editions / Ernst and Sohn (London) 1994.*

MAPPING, MODERNITY AND THE NEW LANDSCAPE

Simon Rycroft

The period 1920 to1970 witnessed far-reaching changes in attitudes toward nature, environment and landscape in Europe, and was characterised by conscious attempts by academics, architects and planners to re-envision human/ environment relationships on the ground. To this end, the project of modernity was clearly central, and the European research project from which this paper arises has covered some theoretical and practical aspects of modern planning.[1] Here, I discuss the vision of a new landscape in Britain; a vision which arose in part from recent technology-led perspectives on nature, and modern mappings of the functioning environment, and was ultimately based upon that reassessment of human/environment relations. This attempt to alter environmental consciousness was in direct opposition to nineteenth-century utilitarian conceptions of nature, and offered an elemental, spiritual and univer- sal conception of the natural world, and ultimately, our place within it. Landscape design, physical planning and education were to make vivid these new understandings, so positioning humans within a functioning environment whose progress and development was to be based upon a natural evolutionary order. The new landscape produced, particularly in the period of post-war reconstruction, was thus to harmonise social order with a conceptual environ- mental or natural order.

An analysis of these modern landscapes is incomplete, however, without an understanding of the basis upon which they were founded; notably, surveying and map- ping. Dudley Stamp's Land Utilisation Survey of Britain, conducted between 1930 and 1934, was one such founda- tion, the results of which were widely used in the emer- gent practice of town and country planning.[2]

In 1930 Stamp set out to homogenise the land use data for Britain, embarking on a project to survey every acre of the nation's land.[3] Previous regional surveys conducted by organisations such as the Le Play Society and the Geo- graphical Associations, whilst pioneering, had only provided fragmentary evidence of land use, its vitality and dynamic.[4] The Land Utilisation Survey of Britain was co-ordinated by regional educational organisations and executed by school pupils. For Stamp, survey was a educational exercise involving accurate observation and map reading. Moreover, since each survey was carried out as part of a national scheme, it inculcated an early appreciation of the importance of the unit in a democracy: land use surveys not only afforded an analysis of how society affects the landscape – a preoccupation for Stamp's holistic appreciation of geography – but also an important exercise in the education of citizens.[5] Combining an educational project with a training in citizenship was basal to any work of national land planning. Through a realisation of the potentialities of their own land and nature, the young surveyors could map a more secure and well-planned future. Carrying out the survey as an educational exercise fulfilled the purpose of engaging people with the land and its problems, an education which would eventually serve the national interest in terms of responsible and ordered planning. Use was made of the maps in the war time drive for efficiency and expansion in agriculture, whilst post-war, the survey laid the foundations for reconstruction.

The Land Utilisation Survey captured and guided changes in the culture of mapping which facilitated different understandings of society, nature and landscape. As aerial photographs surpassed the map as a strategic tool, map usage was extended from primarily military purposes to more popular uses in the early twentieth century. In the inter-war period, the Ordnance Survey introduced leisure maps whose covers depicted cyclists and hikers scanning, from natural promontories, quintessentially English landscapes and reading from the maps which ordered those landscapes. The extension of landscape representation in media like maps and aerial photography ushered in a new experience of landscape, altering popular perspectives from the oblique to the vertical. Despite distancing, the airview of the ground made the importance of land and nature in the evolution of modern society more vivid. Pictures of land and life

and its evolution were all made vivid by the aerial perspective. And the advantages of the airview were deployed by the inter-war town and country planning movement in Britain, prominent members of which were advocates of regional survey. Through their educational work and involvement in youth and rambling groups, they played an important role in the formation and guidance of this new culture of landscape.[6] For Stamp, the results of the survey amplified some of his overriding concerns. The maps demonstrated the misuse of land occurring through *laissez-faire* physical planning around urban areas. London's 'enormous sprawl' stood out as a red tentacled mass, as did to a lesser extent, those of Birmingham, Liverpool, Manchester and the Lancashire cotton towns. The chosen colours accentuated these aspects; garish red and purple for 'unproductive' urban and industrial land and more pastel representative shades of green, yellow and brown for 'productive' rural usages. Urban sprawl, for Stamp was not only inefficient, but also 'unaesthetic': form did not follow function, right use was overridden by misuse.[7]

Stamp concluded that the whole pattern of the land use map of Britain could ultimately be explained by natural physical factors. Despite twentieth-century progress in scientific and technical knowledge, society was still bound by the physical environment. Modern developments, whilst apparently collapsing space, actually accentuated local specialisms. Each region concentrated on the production of the commodity to which their 'natural environment' was best suited. This pointed to the intimate links between society and the land, on which much of Stamp's geography and planning philosophy were based and which the survey intended to elucidate; 'the more man knows of the physical factors and their influence, the more he will act in accordance with them – in other words, the *greater* is the control'.[8]

Stamp's interpretation of land use in Britain found resonance with the post-war planning movement whose immediate concerns were to rescue the notion of planning from its demonic image at the hands of European dictators, and to assert the democratic benefits. Planning was not to take 'blood and soil' as a starting point, but a rational and efficient use of land which recognised local, regional and national allegiances as the building blocks from which a stable democracy could be formed. The landscape of Britain in its orderly appearance, would reflect an equally well-ordered society. This notion took its precedent in the eighteenth century, where the motives for landscape design were not, Stamp felt, based purely upon economics, but on a 'conscious attempt to alter scenery for its own sake', when 'great landowners had no inhibitions about preservation: they were determined to create scenery and . . . so . . . to create beauty'. The twentieth century was less sure of itself, instead, Stamp said, 'we fear the rising tide of change and seek to crystallise and preserve for ever . . . a particular stage in a natural evolution'. Such an aesthetic denied the laws of natural and geological evolution, the land was clothed with a 'living mantle' which constantly altered the appearance of scenery. And the task was to 'direct its growth that we may create beauty, not destroy it'.[9]

To Stamp, planning was an essential element of democracy, and for the balancing of the 'economic and aesthetic needs of the nation'. Despite the synoptic aerial approach of the Land Utilisation survey, such planning was to be rooted at the human scale. Grandiose aerial perspectives and their resultant ambitious plans divorced individuals from environment, tending to destroy local character and nearly all that related to the human scale.

Human-scale modern planning took account of 'functional needs' as the basic factor from which the artist should work with the appliance of art and aesthetics. In this way, the eighteenth-century *spirit* of design could be resurrected, where the landscape and every element within it, from houses to roads, would give visual expression to the living standard, the cultural outlook and the very structure of society. The eighteenth century had much to offer the twentieth-century planner; life itself was 'turned into a piece of art', and that essence was 'distilled into an almost perfect landscape picture'. In sum, the eighteenth-century environment was seen as the product of a 'civilising process' which aimed at 'fusing all elements of the physical world into a unified scheme'.[10] Twentieth-century landscape design was to reflect land ownership and an increasingly *national* identity with its democratic underpinnings. Rather than landed families controlling the nation's heritage, educated citizens well-versed in an understanding of their relationship with the environment

and nature through field study, would, by planning, express this social structure in the landscape.

The aesthetic revolution of the eighteenth century was explained in terms of its revised attitude towards nature, from one which saw it as an 'inversion of the human order, to a perception of the intrinsic harmonies' which provoked love and idealisation. After Newton a more 'intuitive conception' of the universe was seen to develop, one which recognised that nature possessed an order almost inconceivably complex and subtle.[11] In parallel, the planned landscapes of the eighteenth century struck what was seen as an elusive balance between imagination and the intellect, between the spiritual and the rational.

Nineteenth-century mechanisation overwrote the eighteenth-century aesthetic, being 'tragically distant' from cultural activity.[12] Art and architecture in the early twentieth century, a logical conclusion of this distancing, reflected an uncertainty about the material/natural world, a departure from old ideas about matter and form, searching beyond external form to a hidden underlying organisation. In architectural aesthetics, there was a new bias towards an etherealisation of material in suspended structures, paradoxical pinpoint-supported loads and membranes stretched across valleys. But this aesthetic was a recognition of deeper ecological meaning, and an attempt to read logic and order into the natural/material.

If landscape planning was to reflect social structure, then a coherent and ordered social structure was necessary, one which was based upon the diversity of a growing democracy, with an emphasis on progressive change. This diversity operated at all spatial levels from the local to the national, via regional strategic planning: 'By understanding the *genius loci*, new objects expressing a national or regional organisation could be introduced into the local picture, and by skilful juxtaposition with existing objects of local character, could be given a fresh significance in each context'. But over the years, regional identities had shifted; some changed allegiance from village to district, or from district to region, and the planner had to recognise these shifts, and not obstruct them by 'senseless preservation', but assist their acceptance by giving them visual expression.[13] In addition to lessons from eighteenth-century landscape design, relevant new perspectives were to be added – particularly the discovery of new patterns in the microcosmos; new shapes, textures and spatial effects occurring in technics and the revolution in the painter's perspective of the nineteenth and twentieth centuries.

The Land Utilisation Survey, therefore, bore out Stamp's insistence that the form of the landscape, that is, its underlying natural structure, should be reflected in its function, its land use pattern, which in turn was a reciprocal function of social order; he would always stress 'right' use and bemoan misuse, a prejudice which, in its re-evaluation of nature and society resonates with some philosophies of modern design.

In terms of landscape, as a denotation of nature,[14] modern aesthetics made conscious efforts to accommodate existing landscapes, rather than adorning or altering them, abstracting constructions from their settings. At the roots of modern design there are identifiable *elemental* components, shapes and relationships. These natural phenomena were evidenced in society's expanding field of vision during the modern era, from microscopic to macroscopic worlds; atoms and cells to solar systems and galaxies. Modernist aesthetics thus betrayed not only a vision of a particular type of social order, but grounded that social order in conceptual relationship with the natural.

An emphasis on both the elemental and the primitive served to extend the aesthetics of Modernism beyond the local and national to the universal. Rapid advances in science (particularly Einsteinean physics) and technology prompted a re-evaluation of the place of technology in society. The idea of solving the social and ecological consequences of nineteenth-century industrialisation, the nationalist scourge of two wars, and the twentieth century's apparent ignorance of the power technology could hold over society as technocracy, was central to this re-visioning. Technological advances were considered extensions of human bodies and minds, helping to create new, harmonious environments, in which the needs of society complemented the needs of nature. Art, industry and science were urged to co-operate in the formulation of new visions, drawing specifically on the 'newly emerged aspect of nature, hitherto invisible but now revealed by science and technology . . . new vistas of nature which have hardly yet reached our sensibilities'.[15] There was concern that society needed familiarising with these new vistas before it was engulfed and subordinated by them. In short, society needed to be taught critically and visually to appreciate the forms and components of the Modern world and its associated social vision.[16]

The 1951 international New Landscape Exhibition at the Massachusetts Institute of Technology and accompanying volume edited by Gregory Kepes entitled *The New Landscape in Art and Science* (1956), was concerned to do just

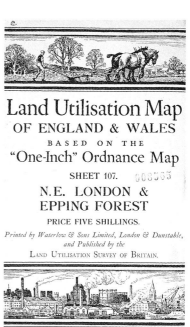

FROM ABOVE: Ellis Martin's cover of the Ordnance Survey Popular edition was a familiar image in the inter-war period. The maps represented and helped guide a culture of nature and landscape; Ellis Martin designed cover of a folded Land Utilisation Map produced for purposes of recreation and general interest and intended to exploit the increased consumption of folded maps in the 1930s

this; to convert this new environment into a human landscape; to generate an appropriate graphic language. To humanise new technologies was a question of scale in relation to the sense experience. Sense experiences, Kepes explained, brought intimacy with nature, humans sensed:

> Form patterns in nature, the sun, the moon, a face, an ear of wheat, the shadow of a tree . . . Stored in memory, re-created in the imagination, they built a feeling of being connected with the physical environment and with other human beings.[17]

It was precisely this human, almost primitivist, connection with nature that Kepes felt needed recovering so that landscape, environment and nature could once again become psychologically calming. Technological advances, or 'the exploded scale of things', produced these new aspects on the natural, from which the development of society seemed out of sync or alienated. But reconnecting the human with the natural was not an abstract process:

> To convert this new environment into a human landscape, we need more than a rational grasp of nature. We need to map the world's new configurations with our senses, dispose our own activities and move-ments in conformity with its rhythms and discover in it potentialities for a richer, more orderly and secure human life.[18]

New technologies, as extensions of ourselves, refined our capacity to observe relationships in nature. To go beyond strict rationalist and scientific forms of observation, the assimilation of the new vision required a meeting of the 'scientist's brain, the poet's heart, the painter's eyes'.[19] This perspective recognised developments in modern physics and non-Euclidean geometry, and attempted to describe reality with more subtlety and power. In the attempt to strengthen contact with nature, science opened up resources for 'new sights and sounds, new tastes and textures': 'If we are to understand the new landscape, we need to touch it with our senses and build the images that will make it ours. For this we must remake our vision'.[20]

As was implicit in Stamp's conception of natural processes, here, the belief in some single mechanism driving the natural world recurs, as Gregory Kepes explained:

> Seen together, aerial maps of river estuaries and road systems, feathers, fern leaves, branching blood vessels, nerve ganglia, electron micrographs of crystals and the tree-like patterns of electrical discharge-figures are connected, although they are different in place, origin and scale. Their similarity of form is by no means accidental. As patterns of energy gathering and energy distribution, they are similar graphs generated by similar processes.'[21]

In this conception, nature represented a harmony of pattern and process, form and function, at all scales. Each scale interlinked with the next forming an integrated and naturally ordered whole, from 'structured molecule, through colloid, cell, organ and individual, to structured society or population, organisation exists in space and time'.[22]

The new landscape was to reflect this modular and proportional order. Like Greek architects or medieval builders who sought to reflect the divine mathematical order of the universe in their constructions, and whose structures demonstrated in their transparent logic a visual manifestation of the perfect correspondence between reason and faith, modern designers were similarly charged. Abstract ideas of form imposed from above thus gave way, in the post-war period to an organic 'form-concept' in which forms evolved from the roots upward, emerging from the properties of the basic units.[23] These forms were thought accurately to reflect and correspond to the mechanisms of nature in their modular, functional linkages, working at an efficient and appropriate scale,

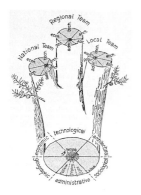

LEFT TO RIGHT: Sir Geoffrey Jellicoe's plans for Oldbury-on-Severn. Austere geometry is off-set by seasonal changes in the character of fields and the sinuous stream which cools the reactor; the conceptual 'Planner's Tree' which demonstrated how a new generation of planners fully versed in the workings and traditions of land and life would harmonise different spatial scales in design considerations

and reaching deep into the primeval subconscious of the human.

The landscape architect Sir Geoffrey Jellicoe, who contributed to debates on post-war reconstruction and planning in Britain, and sat on various forums with Stamp, was much influenced by these aesthetic discourses. In accommodating the 'innumerable activities of the modern world', Jellicoe was concerned to integrate the same new visions of the natural world, to create 'universal gardens' which would evoke transsubjective feelings beyond intellect alone and remind us that 'we are always a part of nature' attuning us to 'that delicate response to nature which has almost passed from our experience'.[24] These emotions, he felt, were 'common from Scandinavia to Australia and Japan, irrespective of race, creed and political belief. Art and instinct reveal the truth but with intellect this is not always so'.[25]

Each new landscape would bypass the rational intellect and reawaken a primitive consciousness of nature. A planned nuclear landscaping project with which Jellicoe was involved, the power station at Oldbury-on-Severn (1960) between Gloucester and Bristol, demonstrates this modern primitivism. Nuclear energy was very much of the new world and therefore, essentially primitive and unclouded by tradition. At Oldbury, the utility of energy production, dictated by scientific necessity – geometric buildings, grids of pipes, wires, pylons – was matched and contrasted by the surrounding agricultural environment: the geometry of the plant was complemented by the angular shapes of the fields and hedgerows, whilst the fourth dimension, time, was represented by the effect of changing seasons on the appearance of the fields, and the flow of water and power in the plant. The infusion of light, the use of water and the proximity of the organic in modern landscape architecture allowed the natural to intersect the modern.[26]

Another nuclear project landscaped by Jellicoe was the particle accelerator at Harwell. Here the mounds, reminiscent of ancient burial sites, echoed the neighbouring Berkshire Downs and were intended to balance spectacular advances in the mechanical sciences with the biological and the primitive. As Jellicoe explained:

In the subterranean laboratories at the foot of the hills the most advanced scientific studies as yet made by man are taking place. The scientist himself will tell you that the splitting of the atom leads to infinity, or as one scientist put it, 'to God'. The mathematical sciences have far outstripped the biological sciences, and this disequilibrium, as we all know, could lead to the eventual destruction of the human race. Opposed to this fearful intellectual development is the human body that is still the same as ever, and within this body, but very deep down under layers of civilisation, are primitive instincts that have remained unchanged.[27]

Through the mounds came this biological association of ideas which would remind us of our humanity, or essential human nature, and thus humanise the technological through landscape.

Jellicoe's vision of naturally functioning landscapes, reflective of new understandings of time, space and technology, found its most lucid form in his design for a future city, Motopia (1968). This expressed an evolutionary vision of which the modern age was a logical end-point: cars, transmitters, houses and roads were all extensions of human functionality in space and could be expressed in the natural modern landscape. Motopia was not the product of the mechanical intellect, but a creative, poetic expression; a natural consequence of the biological evolution of humans. Although its structure was geometrical, a framework of rectangles with circles at the intersections, Motopia rested 'lightly upon the natural landscape', creating a scene similar to that seen 'looking upon landscape through the panes of a Georgian window'.[28] Notionally located near Staines, Motopia would make extensive use of old gravel pits and natural rivers; water would flow 'naturally', unaffected by the geometry of the framework above them.[29] Powered by nuclear energy, Motopia also tapped that most primeval of energy sources.

The functional geometry of Motopia emulated a natural, microscopic cellular form: humans and animals, Jellicoe felt, had an overwhelming urge to return to this 'simple uniformity'. But this need was tempered by Modern aesthetics and an appreciation of the 'stimulus we receive from the beauty of the natural world around us'.[30] Hence, in the architecture of the twentieth-century, in opposition to that of the industrial revolution, the 'counter-industrial revolution', 'endeavoured to conserve nature within [the] architectural environment', not create a programmatic and functional segregation of architecture from the surrounding landscape.[31]

The new landscape as mapped by Dudley Stamp – envisioned by Gregory Kepes et al, and planned by Geoffrey Jellicoe – intended to capture and make vivid a particular mid-twentieth-century sense of social and natural order, one in which society and environment could be harmonised. The discourses of nature, environment and landscape which punctuated these notions clearly underwent transformations in the twentieth century. 'Nature', it seems, is related to the spiritual, primitivist considerations of modern thought and aesthetics, whilst also an object of scientific understanding as 'environment'. 'Landscape' was conflation of the two, a humanised, and visualised, version of 'nature' and 'environment', or as Gregory Kepes phrased it, our natural environment became our human landscape, 'a segment of nature fathomed for us and made home'.[32]

Simon Rycroft is a Lecturer in Human Geography in the School of European Studies at Sussex University. His research interests include the geographies of the underground press in Britain and America in the 1960s, and environmental meanings in the post-war period.

Notes

1 This research was sponsored by the European Commission's SEER programme under the title 'Nature, Environment, Landscape: European Attitudes and Discourses in the Modern Period (1920-70), with Particular Attention to Water Regulation' (contract number EV5V-CT92-0151). Along with research from Swedish, Italian and Danish consortium members, an earlier version of this paper was presented at the 1995 annual conference of the Institute of British Geographers at Northumbria University.

2 For biographical material on Dudley Stamp's life and work see RO Buchanan, 'The Man and his Work' in *Land Use and Resources: Studies in Applied Geography*, IBG Special Publication (London) 1968; MJ Wise, 'Sir Dudley Stamp: His Life and Times' in *Land Use and Resources: Studies in Applied Geography*; MJ Wise, 'Three Founder Members of the IBG: R Ogilvie Buchanan, Sir Dudley Stamp, SW Wooldridge: A Personal Tribute', *Transactions of the Institute of British Geographers*, NS Vol 8, No. 4, 1983.

3 The Land Utilisation Survey was produced in map form and in a series of regional monographs edited by Stamp. For accounts of the survey and its conduct, see LD Stamp, *The Land of Britain: Its Use and Misuse*, third edition, Longmans, Green & Co Ltd, with Geographical Publications Ltd, 1962; 'Nationalism and land utilisation in Britain', *The Geographical Journal*, Vol 27, No. 1, pp11-20; 'Land Utilisation Survey of Britain', *The Geographical Review*, Vol 24, 1937, pp646-50; 'Planning the land for the future', *Science*, 1934, Vol 80, No. 2084, 1934, pp510-12. See also S Rycroft and D Cosgrove, 'Mapping the Modern Nation: Dudley Stamp and the Land Utilisation Survey of Britain', *History Workshop Journal*, Vol 40, Autumn 1995, pp91-105.

4 Consider, for example, the work of David Matless on these earlier surveys and the geographers, planners and sociologists who conducted them: D Matless, *Ordering the Land: The 'Preservation' of the English Countryside 1918-1939*, unpublished PhD thesis, (University of Nottingham) 1989; 'Nature, the Modern and the Mystic: Tales from Early Twentieth Century Geography', *Transaction of the Institute of British Geographers*, NS, Vol 16, 1991, pp272-86; 'Regional Surveys and Local Knowledges: The geographical imagination in Britain, 1918-39', *Transactions of the Institute of British Geographers*, Vol 17, 1992.

5 On Stamp's concept of geographical study see L D Stamp, *Applied Geography*, Penguin Books (Harmondsworth) 1960.

6 D Matless, 'Regional Surveys and Local Knowledges: The geographical imagination in Britain, 1918-39', *Transactions of the Institute of British Geographers*, Vol 17, 1992, p5.

7 LD Stamp, *The Land of Britain: Its Use and Misuse*, p440.

8 *Ibid*, p41.

9 LD Stamp, *Man and the Land*, New Naturalist Series, Collins

(London) 1955, *xiii.*

10 GM Kallman and IRM McCallum, 'Design', in IRM McCallum (ed), *Physical Planning*, The Architectural Press (London) 1945, pp243-44.

11 *Ibid*, pp253-54.

12 *Ibid*, p259.

13 *Ibid*, pp267-68.

14 Consider KR Olwig in 'Sexual Cosmology: Nation and Landscape at the Conceptual Interstices of Nature and Culture, or: What does Landscape Really Mean?' *Landscape: Politics and Perspective*, Berg (Oxford) 1993, pp307-43.

15 G Kepes, *The New Landscape in Art and Science*, p17.

16 These discourses are set out in many texts on modern design and aesthetics. See for example G Kepes, *The New Landscape in Art and Science*; GA Jellicoe, *Studies in Landscape Design*, Oxford University Press (Oxford)1960; GA Jellicoe, *Studies in Landscape Design Volume II*, Oxford University Press (Oxford) 1966; GA Jellicoe, *The Landscape of Man: Shaping the Environment from Prehistory to the Present*, Thames and Hudson (London) 1975.

17 G Kepes, *The New Landscape in Art and Science*, Paul Theobald & Co (Chicago) 1956, p18.

18 *Ibid*, p19.

19 *Ibid*, pp21-28.

20 *Ibid*, p20.

21 G Kepes, 'Analogue Metaphor', in *The New Landscape in Art and Science*, p260.

22 RW Gerard, 'Design and Function in the Living' in G Kepes, *The New Landscape in Art and Science*, pp277-79.

23 G Kepes, 'Symmetry Proportion Module' in *The New Landscape in Art and Science*, p352.

24 GA Jellicoe, *Studies in Landscape Design*, p30.

25 GA Jellicoe, *The Landscape of Man: Shaping the Environment from Prehistory to the Present*, Thames and Hudson (London) 1975, p345.

26 Details of Jellicoe's Oldbury design can be found in GA Jellicoe, *Studies in Landscape Design Volume II*, pp7-16.

27 GA Jellicoe, *Studies in Landscape Design: Volume II*, p14.

28 GA Jellicoe, *Motopia: A Study in the Evolution of Urban Landscape*, Frederick A Praeger (New York) 1961, p12.

29 Jellicoe explored the theme of water in design with his wife in GA Jellicoe and S Jellicoe, *Water: The Use of Water in Landscape Architecture*, Adam & Charles Black (London) 1971.

30 GA Jellicoe, *Motopia*, p47.

31 M Spens, 'Admirable Jellicoe', *Architectural Review*, Vol 86, No. 1,111, 1989, p86.

32 G Kepes, *The New Landscape in Art and Science*, p18.

ABOVE AND CENTRE: Jellicoe's landscaping for the particle accelerator at Harwell. In form the hills are true to the region by echoing the nearby Berkshire Downs, but also highlight the primeval nature of nuclear experimentation, being reminiscent of ancient burial mounds. In both senses, the mechanical is humanised by the ecological; BELOW: detail of the 'future city' Motopia designed by Jellicoe, Ove Arup and Mills for the Glass Age Development Committee of Messrs Pilkington Brothers Limited. Nature and landscape flow through the built environment which itself takes a modular form inspired by similar forms seen in modern vistas of nature

THE SURVIVAL OF LANCELOT 'CAPABILITY' BROWN

John Phibbs

Two hundred years ago Herefordshire squires Richard Payne Knight and Uvedale Price launched their attack on Capability Brown, and in doing so established a caricature of his style that is still current. The man responsible for embedding this caricature into our culture is Humphry Repton, whose weak defence only served to damn Brown further. Repton's *Sketches and Hints* was to have been published in 1794, and it seems fitting to review the effect that these three 'assassins' have had on Brown's reputation.

I hope to look at each of their criticisms in the light of what we know of Brown's work and contrast them with comments made by authors more sympathetic to Brown. The most important of these are Thomas Whately (a close friend of Cobham's nephew, George Grenville, for whom Brown worked at Wotton) and RL Girardin, the Vicomte d'Ermenonville. I would be happy to believe that both these men had discussed landscape with Brown. Other useful sources are William Mason and William Marshall, although in both cases I suspect that their own views on landscape qualified their understanding of Brown.

I have also used both editions of George Mason's *Essay on Design in Gardening*. It seems to me that George Mason must have met Brown between writing the two editions of the essay, and rather admired him, even though he could not bring himself to say so. He certainly seems to have admired landscapes without realising that Brown had worked on them.

The attacks made by the assassins may be confronted, but since Brown left no detailed written theory, this can only be done by reference to Brown's work – and there is no complete list of what he did, or even locations of his work. Generally speaking, therefore, we have no way of knowing whether or not Brown advised on a particular planting, or of knowing exactly when it was put in. I have visited approximately seventy per cent of the landscapes attributed to Brown, persuading myself that elements of design that crop up repeatedly in these landscapes are likely to be from his hand, or approved by him. However, I am aware that we know far too little to make any direct attribution, and I have tried throughout to refer more generally to 'Brownian style', 'Brown landscapes', and 'Brown's work'. However much it may appear to the contrary, my own interest is not so much in Brown himself as in the idea that the philosophy and practice of the most influential and best-loved school of eighteenth-century landscape design is entirely foreign to us and has been misunderstood for 200 years.

My approach is also at odds with the idea of cultural landscape; defined by ICOMOS as 'the conviction at dealing with landscapes starts from a consideration of human values, and that there are no objective criteria for determining importance'. I have read Brown's landscapes as primarily aesthetic in intent, and regard his work as the best of its type. It follows that the landscapes on which he worked in a significant way are likely to be more important and more valuable than others designed by lesser figures.

Time and the Assassins

Let us be aware of the threat to Brown. His reputation is unassailable; with Le Nôtre he is the most famous gardener in the world. His name is indelibly associated with the great aristocratic landowners of the eighteenth century and with their parks: Alnwick, Blenheim, Bowood, Chatsworth, Grimsthorpe, Harewood, Longleat, Petworth, Tottenham and so forth. These places are celebrated in photographs and pictures wherever English culture is discussed. They are hardly representative of his work, and one consequence of their international iconic importance is that planning authorities tend to dismiss smaller places as if they were lesser, or indeed as if Brown could not have worked at them because they do not look like Petworth. Yet Berrington, Beechwood, Coopersale, Hawnes, King's Weston, Shortgrove, Warnford, Youngsbury and many places like them, are not comparable with the great deer parks. They were laid out for different purposes and for a different kind of management.

At present it seems to me that more of Brown's landscapes are under threat than, say, Repton's, simply because the range of work that Brown undertook was so great and his range of solutions so sophisticated. Here then is one kind of assassination.

Where these smaller landscapes which make up the bulk of his commissions do survive, they have often been 'Brownised'. We find them swept neurotically clean of bushes, bumps and trees and re-created in the pattern of the assassins' caricature: we have uncritically accepted this caricature, but we have also accepted that Brown is a great landscape gardener, and this leaves us reproducing (and having to regard as beautiful) the monotonous formulaic landscapes that Price and Knight set up for our scorn. Here is a second kind of assassination.

There occurred a third kind: the remarkable currency that Price and Knight achieved with their vilification of Brown, both in their own day and ever since. It would be of value for the historical record to redress the balance even if no Brown landscapes survived today.

I do not think it would be controversial to say that Brown's intentions were primarily aesthetic, since most of his planting and earthworks do not make sense as commercial forestry or farm management.

There is also general acceptance for the view that what he did worked. I suspect that Brown himself would have been dissatisfied if his landscapes had not provided sufficient paddocks for the stock, hay for the horses, vegetables and flowers for the house, or if they had required continual maintenance.

Conclusions

There is only one idea at the root of this research. As a result of things that happened at the end of the eighteenth century (the Picturesque movement of course and Repton's works, but also perhaps political and social changes brought on by the French Revolution), we no longer understand the aesthetics and intentions of mid-eighteenth-century landscapes; we now see them through the eyes of the late eighteenth century, through a 'Regency filter'. I first presented this idea in the article in *Garden History* on Swedish gardens. While the argument was confined to the pleasure ground, the idea was supported by a good deal of documentary evidence.

Today we know next to nothing about how Brown operated his business or what he was trying to do – and yet we are in the middle of a vast programme of replanting parks, brought on by the great storms of 1987 and 1990. How can we expect to get this right with so little understanding? It should not be a crime to admit that we do not understand eighteenth-century landscape, and we should hold back from completely replanting parks and gardens of this kind until we have learnt more about them.

It is a poor defence that repudiates every criticism but proposes no alternative interpretation of its hero. Nonetheless, this is the path that I have taken. My aim is to record the enduring triumph of the Picturesque movement and the assassins: their interpretation of Brown has governed our reading of his work for 200 years, and it has suffered as a result. I have suggested that changes in land management and animal husbandry between 1770 and 1790 may have prejudiced the judgement of the assassins.

I may be unusual in regarding Repton as one of the assassins: two of his more outspoken unpublished attacks are to be found in the Longleat and Thoresby Red Books. Repton's work is tremendously difficult to characterise: some associate Repton with the Picturesque movement and argue that the two are hard to distinguish; others associate him with Brown, for the same reason. Yet most people would say that there are profound differences between Brown and the picturesques. I can show that Brown and the Picturesque movement had a surprising amount in common, both in philosophy and technique; and that Repton was the odd one out.

I am not alone in this view – here is William Marshall, for example, in his review of Price's *Essays*: 'our Author, in effect, has hitherto been preaching what Mr Brown has practised – (some small differences excepted)', (Marshall, 1795, p134). Both Brown and the theorists of the movement believed that landscaping was about making pictures, though Brown believed that a considerable expenditure was often required, both to bring out the best in Nature and to conceal the worst in man. The Reverend William Gilpin, a precursor of the Picturesque movement, showed how close the two styles were, in his important description of the potential of Keswick (Gilpin, 1776, Vol 1 p161): 'It might be rendered more accessible – it might be cleared of deformities – it might be planted – and it might be

decorated.' The passage deserves reading in full, for it also illustrates his unquestioned sense of the importance of the views out. I hope my research will stimulate an appraisal of Brown's style to complement the monumental work of cataloguing and collation that underlies Dorothy Stroud's biography; in order to speed this appraisal on its way, I shall conclude with some points not previously raised here.

Notes for Further Research

I have deliberately kept references to Nature to a minimum. Nature was paramount in eighteenth-century aesthetics and gardening. For that reason it was interpreted in many different ways, and as a result it seems to have become too difficult a concept to help with the interpretation of landscape. Basil Willey gave a very good overview of the problem (Willey, 1946).

Despite the assassins' talk of formulae, it does not seem possible to me to characterise Brown's work on the evidence of a single county. One associates different parts of England with different types of Brown; lakes in Warwickshire and villas in the home counties, for example. There are many reasons for this: the topography, geology, climate, patterns of landholding and agriculture, economic history and landed interest, must all have contributed to the geographical variation within Brown's work, and I would add to that the likelihood that one of his foremen may have worked on several adjacent landscapes at the same time and thus given them similar detailing.

There will always be a place for regional studies, but the risk then remains that we shall continue to compare every Brownian landscape with the local 'giant' – thus one might find oneself comparing Cadland or Warnford with Highclere when all three places are entirely different and can only be evaluated by looking outside Hampshire.

No one would deny that Brown is the most famous landscape gardener that England has produced, or that his work is classic, in the sense that every gardener since his day has had to respond to it. However, it seems that (Dorothy Stroud excepted) there has been remarkably little research done on Brown.

Susanne Seymour, among others, has pointed out that the lack of decent documentation and the geographical distribution of Brown's *oeuvre* mitigate against this, but very good work is being done on a number of his contemporaries (Emes, Richmond, the Whites and Woods for example), and it still seems to me a remarkable blank spot. Most scholars take as read the caricature of Brown put out by the assassins, and this seems to me to undermine their conclusions.

I believe I can give as an example Nigel Everett's *A Tory View of Landscape* (1994) without fear of offence, because I have found it so useful in writing this paper, not least for its exemplary synthesis of a wide range of eighteenth-century writing. His theme is an exploration of two attitudes to landscape: the Tory (benevolent landlords, well-housed tenantry, distaste for Adam Smith and 'new money', associated with a certain kind of civic liberty and characterised by Squire Allworthy in *Tom Jones*) and the Whig (improvement, enclosure, clearances, village destruction, reform, Capability Brown, unbridled liberty).

To demonstrate Brown's place in this theory, Everett distils Price's *Essays* into two or three pages, without comment (an approach also used by Christopher Hussey when he defended Brown in the introduction to the 1984 edition of Dorothy Stroud's book). Of course, the assassins' caricature perfectly answers Everett's thesis, but it weakens the book because Brown worked for almost all the social reformers (that is, the Tories) that he mentions. Many of his examples are derived from contributors to Thomas Bernard's reports for the Society for Bettering the Condition and Increasing the Comforts of the Poor; his list includes Conyers (Copped Hall); Egremont (Petworth); Harcourt (Nuneham); Hardwicke (Wimpole); Rutland (Belvoir); Shelburne (Bowood); Winchilsea (Lapidge, at any rate, worked at Burley). This criticism does not actually affect the value of Everett's book, which depends not on what Brown did, but on what he was thought to have done. In fact, the book becomes more interesting if we consider that the entire 'whig' tradition of landscape and improvement, though current even in the eighteenth century, had no basis in fact.

Contemporary pictures provide one accessible source for eighteenth-century landscape: art historians would do garden history a service if they could sift out those that are topographically accurate and then ask of them how these landscapes were managed: where are the fences, how is the grass kept down, are the large animals in the foreground cows or oxen, where was the artist, what are the iconographies of deer, cows and sheep, and do they change in the late eighteenth century?

I am curious about pictures with haymaking in the foreground of a big house, but before rushing to impose on these their social, literary and political context it would be helpful to ask where the family was at the time. And what did the hayfield look like during the rest of the year

ABOVE: The dairy on the edge of the pleasure ground at Wynnstay, Clwyd, is a theatrical sham; it is strapped on to a gardener's cottage. The sham building is a common device; Brown's approach to landscape was theatrical and we should expect to find structures of wood and painted canvas in his work; BELOW: Wimpole in Cambridgeshire is a fine example of a landscape that appears conventionally Brownian. The south front is dominated by Bridgeman's longest extant avenue, left untouched by Brown. The earthworks of an earlier avenue are visible running inside Bridgeman's. These are not only of interest in themselves as a record of medieval agriculture, but are also significant as a part of the designed landscape – Brown must have seen them and elected to retain them

– why was the painting made at just this moment? Perhaps these pictures were commissioned to illustrate that clever Mr Brown's new style of parkland management; perhaps we should be asking why so few pictures of great houses have haycarts in the foreground.

Eighteenth-century bank accounts provide another relatively accessible source for Brown's work, and Peter Willis has shown how much can be gleaned from these. By comparing them with estate accounts it may be possible to establish who was paid (Brown, his foreman, estate workers, or gangs) and how they were paid (through a bank or direct) and thus to gain a sense of the scale of Brown's involvement. We may also begin to distinguish works that Brown directed himself; those directed by each of his foremen; those carried out by gangs of men under an owner's control; those that were carried out over time, as part of an estate's general management, perhaps with occasional visits by Brown.

We should also look at our records of payments made to Brown, for example round payments in numbers of guineas (particularly 30, 50, 60, 80 or 100) may indicate an agreement to produce a plan only, or a plan with a number of visits charged at Brown's daily rate. King's Weston is a good example of this.

Brown's surviving plans are a less reliable guide to what he did. These are often thought of as a full and accurate record of his proposals, but they are not: firstly because they usually do not show drives or earthworks, and secondly because any plan is likely to be modified in the execution – but Brown does not seem to have felt the need to produce a new drawing to record every change.

There should be some way of recording the large scale, evenly graded earthworks that typify Brown's work. At present it is often difficult to believe that what one is looking at is an earthwork rather than the natural. From such a record one should be able to estimate where and how much soil was cut away and deposited, often over several hundred acres. Chatsworth, Stapleford and Swynnerton, are useful parks to begin with. These three have Brownian earthworks overlaid on earlier forms which survive in good condition. This makes it easy to pick out, and have faith in, the eighteenth-century contribution. One might then progress to sites like Highclere and Alnwick, which have equally complex earthworks without such a clear palimpsest.

Once such records have been made, it should be easier to create a vocabulary to describe Brown's earthworks and to understand what they were intended to do. We might begin to look at the percentage of the parkland acreage that has earthworks on it as a guide to the value of conserving a site. It might even be possible to consider the reinstatement of Brownian and earlier earthworks in parkland – particularly where, as on the ploughed, featureless, grass hill behind Audley End, twentieth-century landscape has produced a landscape that is really 'bare and bald'.

Where Brownian landscaping is to be destroyed, the planting and earthworks could be recorded before they are 'swept away'. At the very least the modified land-form and the planting could be recorded and described with a video camera, so that future generations will have a data bank to use for the study and management of these landscapes.

The following is a list of Brown landscapes that seem to be under threat: Adderbury, Oxon; Ampthill, Beds; Ashburnham, Sussex; Benham, Berks; Berrington, Hereford and Worcester; Bowood, Wilts; Burton, Sussex; Caversham, Berks; Chalfont, Bucks; Church Stretton, Shrops; Cole Green, Herts; Combe Abbey, Warks; Compton Verney, Warks; Coopersale, Essex; Copped Hall, Essex; Croome, Hereford and Worcester; Digswell, Herts; Ditton, Berks; Dornford, Oxon; Escot, Devon; Flambards, Mddx; Gatton, Surrey; Hallingbury, Essex; Harleyford, Bucks; Hawnes, Beds; Hewell Grange, Hereford and Worcester; Himley, Staffs; The Hoo, Herts; Ingestre, Staffs; Kelston, Avon; King's Weston, Avon; Latimer, Bucks; Longleat, Wilts; Maiden Erlegh, Berks; Mamhead, Devon; Melton Constable, Norfolk; Milton Abbey, Dorset; Moor Park, Herts; Newton, Avon; Nuneham, Oxon; Patshull, Staffs; Paultons, Hants; Peper Harow, Surrey; Petworth, Surrey; Pishiobury, Herts; Porter's, Herts; Radley, Oxon; Sandleford, Berks; Sharpham, Devon; Stanmore, Mddx; Stoke Park, Bucks; Stapleford, Leics; Stoke Place, Bucks; Testwood, Hants; Trentham, Staffs; Valence, Kent; Wardour, Wilts; Warwick, Warks; Wycombe, Bucks; Wynnstay, Clwyd; Youngsbury, Herts. This is a short and by no means exhaustive list (my first had over eighty sites on it), and of course it is subjective. I have tried to include places that are in the grip of, or are very likely to fall into the grip of, irreversible change: some are being built on, subject to planning applications, losing their earthworks to golf courses, and some are under management that no longer has the same interest in farming that Brown had (schools and golf courses fall into this category). One does not have to be elitist to subscribe to this list: there is no reason why a golf course should not be laid out on a Brown landscape; indeed surprisingly few have been and it could be argued that many golf courses have protected landscapes that might otherwise have been destroyed (examples include Addington, Surrey; Ashridge, Herts; Audley End, Essex; Bowood, Wilts; Chalfont, Herts; Cowdray, Sussex; Edgbaston, Warks; Flambards, Mddx; Himley, Staffs; Ingestre, Staffs; Langley, Bucks; Moor Park, Herts; Patshull, Staffs; Radley, Oxon; Stoke Park, Bucks; Stoke Green, Bucks). However, it is a matter for concern when such developments take place without the slightest attention to Brown, and certain combinations of development are particularly worrying (for example a golf course on a Brown landscape that has earthworks).

Landscapes owned by organisations such as schools and golf clubs may provide a steady financial return and are therefore unlikely to be brought to the attention of conservationists, yet because so many of them provide access of one kind or another to the public, these landscapes are most deserving of help.

Repairing Brown Landscapes

While restoration in the strict sense is seldom possible, it is a pity that today there are so few Brownian landscapes that come close to realising his intentions. We are particularly lacking in certain categories of landscape: a ruin, such as Roche Abbey, a pleasure ground like Eywood, or farmed parkland like Berrington – all would be welcome; indeed, the National Trust do intend to put back what they can of the Brownian parkland at Berrington.

Current policy would have us replant to the latest major phase of a landscape's development. Brown is particularly vulnerable to this because his landscapes depend on symmetries and scarcely perceptible vistas, created by bays in the planting and slight changes of level. These are the vistas that are always blocked by later (often commemorative) planting, but once they have gone we cannot pretend that the structure of the composition is still Brownian.

Whatever the exact purpose of Brown's direct and principal approaches, they are an important part of his design and he spent a lot of money on them. A car park at the centre of the landscape near the house obviously destroys the setting of the house, and also contrives to focus the landscape on the house in a way that Brown deliberately sought to avoid. Furthermore, it brings visitors to the house in the wrong way.

Whatever else Brown was, he was an improver; like any other eighteenth-century manager, he would have devoted a good deal of time to procuring fertiliser, whether lime, marl or manure. Like any other manager he would have been distressed to see anything but a grass or grass and clover mix in the lawns about the house. Arthur Young and William Marshall in their accounts for the Board of Agriculture often refer to the importance of fertilising. Today we are encouraged to manage grassland so as to increase its value for nature conservation. The herb-rich sward may be appropriate in some parts of a Brownian landscape but it should not be developed in all of it.

For some reason we tend to ignore ridings as an element of the designed landscape. Yet these, more than any other kind of lowland landscape, could provide the Holy Grail of a form of conservation that offers access to the countryside but does not impede agriculture.

Repton frequently commented that he could do more good to a landscape by cutting a few trees down than by planting a hundred. The same is true today – particularly with Brown landscapes where landlords seem to be so drawn to planting trees in the vistas – however, Brownian landscapes do need very carefully positioned planting near the house. Wherever possible we should integrate the management of parkland and pleasure grounds made between 1750 and 1830: Brown's intention was to make one flow into the other.

On tree use I have suggested that Brown used a wide range of short-term planting for instant effect. Trees included alder, willow, poplar and conifers. We are often reluctant to use these genera.

'Informal' is one word that should never be used in connection with Brown. It is particularly dangerous if replanting is under consideration because it can be interpreted to mean that, in large areas of the landscape, the detailed setting out and distribution of trees is left to the contractor or forester. We could do worse than mull over Brown's discussion with Hannah More: his metaphor was literary, but he did not wave his hand across the landscape and say 'Here is my three-volume novel, there my epic poem, and beyond it my grand opera', instead he spoke in terms of commas and colons – his design was all in the detail.

John Phibbs is the principal of Debois Landscape Survey Group, a consultancy, founded in 1979, that specialises in the management and conservation of historic landscapes.

A NEW KIND OF PARK

DIANA BALMORI

The Gwynns Falls Trail in Baltimore represents the recovery of a modest piece of a linear landscape. In the past, these strips of land were ignored or put to a utilitarian purpose but are now being converted into a new kind of public entity. Gwynns Falls Trail is not a true trail, it is one of a new breed of park – the *linear park*. A newly emerging species, it was originally generated in response to the large-scale abandonment of railway lines across the United States, and has since spread along utility corridors and streams. It is a new form whose possibilities have not yet been fully explored. It may now be timely and useful to summarise its main characteristics and indicate its greater appropriateness and promise to our times and culture than the traditional central urban parks of the Olmsted era. However, it must be stated that these new parks inherit from the famous parks of the nineteenth century the symbolic importance of an embodiment of our civic ideals.

The original American park movement emerged in response to industrialisation and to the dense industrial hub cities it created. The movement established the 'idea' of parks – not piazzas, public squares or esplanades, but central urban parks – as both the best response to the new conditions and as the ideal public space for American society. These parks came to represent physical and spiritual health, natural beauty and democracy. Today, after several revolutions in our society's modes of trans-portation and in a culture quite different, the park – now in its new linear form – continues to attract the idealists in American society as a powerful medium in which to articulate their ideals for, and innovative refigurations of, public space. It is always important to observe in a society the icons by which it chooses to represent itself. The way a society defines its public space, as the embodiment of its deepest civic ideals, provides richer ground for analysis than will many of its powerful institutions. Today's linear park has sparked the first truly widespread citizen move-ment about public space since the 1830-60 great park era, drawing the same broad-based grass-roots idealism and

LEFT TO RIGHT: Map of entry points; design of entry points is critical to the success of the linear park to make it memorable and to represent the goals of the park as a whole. This entry point builds a miniaturised walk-in landscape of the watershed of the whole park; bridges

support that the nineteenth-century urban parks did.

What are the main characteristics, then, of this new ideal public space, the linear park? It is, above all, the creation of a dynamic set of connections rather than of a destination. It responds to a new stage in our thinking about transportation and to the peripatetic spirit that has long characterised American life. The linear park opens pathways to diverse neighbourhoods and new recreational spaces and experiences of nature; it invites exploration of alternate modes of transport and of cultural resources. It weaves connections between city and suburb, suburb and country, between nature and culture, and among people of different origin, age or sex. It is an answer to the increasing cultural isolation and physical separation in which we often find ourselves.

Practical park management considerations, such as maintenance, safety and accessibility, also argue in favour of the linear park. This new form of public recreational space – a corridor of modest width – provides maximum neighbourhood and public accessibility and a continuous open channel for maintenance and surveillance. Because of the form's permeability and continuity, the linear park avoids the hazards occasioned by the isolation and disconnection so frequently encountered in many traditional urban parks.

Linear parks reveal a new narrative of the American landscape they inscribe themselves upon, and, in so doing, forecast a change in the nature of our sense of national identity. In initiating and providing for a new way of understanding our modes of transportation, linear parks assume the narrative power that once belonged to three earlier forces that shaped American landscape and identity. The first of these was the railway which transformed the character of America in its westward expansion to the Pacific Ocean. Frederick Turner made of this narrative a theory of history – that of the last frontier. The second of these forces was that of the automobile and its network of highways. This was the narrative of the 'open road' popularised by Jack Kerouac's *On the Road*, Hollywood's

Easy Rider and innumerable other movies. The airplane and the new view of landscape it revealed introduced the third narrative.

The railroad revolutionised the American landscape; its narrative involved the displacement and eradication of the last inner wilderness, refuge to many nations of Native Americans, many species of wildlife and many ecosystems, at the same time spurring the creation of towns, zoned landscapes and the metropolis. This first narrative broke out from the east, whereas the second came sprawling out of the midwest, from Detroit. Gasoline-powered vehicles and the asphalt and concrete ribbons that rolled out from under their wheels, spread city and industry outside the metropolis and created isolated suburbs, industrial parks, strip development, and an economy based on the use of cheaper land. The land once swallowed by agricultural acreage was now consumed by speculative developments.

This change in our perception of landscape was soon succeeded by yet another with the invention of the airplane and its industry, this time rising out of the west. The airplane revealed more than just a change in perspective: it revealed patterns of agriculture, of geology, of earlier landscape forms and of the relation of towns and country. The first two narratives had expanded the sense of a nation, giving the experience of the landscape to a broader portion of the population; with the rise of the aerospace age, a new sense of space diminished the magnitude and significance of national boundaries.

Our present narrative returns us to a level of motion that precedes our industrial narratives. The linear park, such as Gwynns Falls Trail, offers an inner frontier unimagined by Turner or by the New Frontier advocates of outer-space exploration: its trails return control of the land to us as individuals and as a people. This has far-reaching consequences: the linear park represents a movement towards a re-envisioning of our own communities. It transforms both the metropolis of the railway age and the suburbs of the highway age. These trails mend the community fabric by drawing people together along a common way, as once town streets did before the automobile. They return to us the significance of context, of the contiguity of places, and of the life that converges along them. People can again interact with each other and with the land they inhabit.

In a time when open land has been voraciously consumed by suburbs and unending construction, the linear park extends a continuous line of living and healing tissue, a habitat corridor which fosters life rather than expanding this corrosive sub-urbanisation, and projects a continuous garden through city, suburb and farmland. In effect, the direct experience of the landscape, often lost in the industrial age, is, for the first time, recaptured.

It is not simply a modest tweaking of our concept of park, that our fourth narrative poses, but a major reconstitution of the way we use space and time and the means by which we transport ourselves. We cannot imagine now the consequences of this revision. By transforming these corridors into havens for pedestrians and cyclists, we no longer relegate ourselves to the sidewalks of highways, but become the shaping force of the corridor, now free of all machines fuelled by other than human energy.

Because economics follow people, this new park system, whose measure is human motion, promises to be economically productive. Even as the railroad and highway before it, the linear park energises areas around it. Though it invites dense development along its route's edges, we have the opportunity with the linear park to think how we wish to implement and direct such growth. Even as nineteenth-century parks did, the linear park can increase land values and attract premium residential areas around its perimeters. At the same time, however, the continuity and length of these corridors also lend themselves to a variety of commercial and institutional uses. And further, we can discern a political potential in these parks as new avenues to community empowerment.

The originality of the linear park must be expressed immediately and boldly. We must not bury it in ideals and agendas of the past. In form and approach, I think it is not too idealistic to propose that they be built using clean energy sources, that they be drained, planted, built and maintained in a way that recovers for us a healthy environment, that they be reliable refuges in which nature can function according to its principles. They should be places in which the living population of plants, animals and people can survive independently and regenerate themselves: places in which water can run pure and be fished or waded in without endangering our health. We can, in this modest strip of land, create a blueprint for the life we wish for ourselves.

The commitment to working with the many diverse communities along these linear corridors is not a mere reiteration of the democratic ideals that propelled the American park movement. The new park does cover ground already passed over, but it encounters and engages along its way new voices which were neither attended to nor engaged before. The master plan for Gwynns Falls Trail is part of this emerging vision of the linear park. Every element of its design is meant to embody the overall idea. It belongs to this new generation of American parks cast in the revolutionary role of knitting together pieces of the urban and suburban fabric and transforming the experience of life in an American city.

Because our parks embody the ideals of American life more than our cities, the transformation of the physical body of the city is more readily achieved by the creation and introduction of the new linear park into the city than by any direct treatment of the city as a whole. The park in America has always given public expression to the democratic aspirations of our society, to its need for places of beauty, and to its attachment to landscape as part of everyday life.

The ideals of health, beauty and democracy of the nineteenth-century park movement still shape our idea of the park, though they have been translated into our twentieth-century vocabulary. Health, as we now understand it, is the health of the ecosystem – its ability to sustain its own life. Beauty we translate now as the voice of art, in shaping nature jointly in environmental and aesthetic ways. Democracy is translated into an equality of access to all regardless of age, gender or origin.

Goals

The Gwynns Falls Trail is a fourteen-mile trail running along a stream (Gwynns Falls) that ends at Harbor Place in the heart of downtown Baltimore. The master plan seeks to create a public space which embraces the following goals:

- To create connections among diverse neighbourhoods along the trail and with the natural and human resources of the city as a whole.
- To reveal the character of the watershed by making manifest its history, its nature and the living community it sustains.
- To create a hierarchy of access points based on their relative physical and cultural importance and provide

for a clear sense of orientation at each of them.

- To draw attention to the whole body of the trail, which is a stream, and its watershed, and to heal it from its degradation in the industrial age by using and displaying ways of regenerating the life of the watershed.

- To develop and engage our evolving twenty-first-century understanding of nature as a complete ecosystem capable of sustaining and reproducing itself.

- To create a human sculpture by linking the different bodies governing water issues (such as the COE, EPA, DNR, SOS, and Save the Chesapeake Bay) to form a coalition for the Gwynns Falls Watershed.

- To illustrate a process in each design which changes the manner in which parks and cities are designed and which will establish an ethical and environmentally sound set of procedures for the design and construction of such a trail; a process which eliminates the use of pollutants, which creates jobs for surrounding communities, which can be integrated into the education of those around it, and which is, at all times, inclusive.

- To seek designs which are easy to manage and ensure the safety of trail users. Emphasis in the master plan is placed on the way in which the ideas about the trail are realised. The emphasis lies in the way that the linear park integrates the surrounding neighbourhoods, in the way that it engages the co-operative participation of the different authorities and governing bodies to rehabilitate this stream and trail, and in the way that it draws upon the different disciplines to give form to its ultimate design. Our team for the Gwynns Falls Trail was made up of the following members: *Team Leader:* Diana Balmori, project leader, Balmori Associates; *Balmori Associates Team:* Diana Balmori, principal; Ana Maria Torres, project manager; William Coyne, designer; Fran Leadon, designer; *Design Team:* Diana Balmori, landscape and urban designer; Paul Barten, hydrologist; Jonathan Fishman, architect; Kristen McDougall, graphic designer; Edward Orser, urban historian; Meg Webster, environmental sculptor. The gathering of these different resources is not an afterthought, but a determining element of the design itself. The clients for this project were the Trust for Public Land and the City of Baltimore.

- To clearly manifest the restoration process of the entire watershed from its decay as an industrial-age dumping ground and sewer channel to a thickly planted, water-cleaning environment. To this end, the design includes areas for collecting trash and devices, to be located at the most offensive outlets in the stream, for aerating and cleaning the wetland water that will be designed in an aesthetically-pleasing form. New bridges across the stream are also planned which will serve to make manifest the importance of water and provide a place from which to enjoy the stream. One of the bridges will house a cafe, another, a fishing set-up, and, on another, will stretch a planted trellis archway.

- This vision stands, as it were, on the shoulders of an earlier vision that was created for public space in Baltimore in 1904 by the Olmsted Brothers at the request of Baltimore's Municipal Art Society. This Olmsted document must be the starting place for any new plan for public space in Baltimore precisely because of its broad vision and its understanding of the park as an integral part of our cities.

I have delved into such detail about a particular new park's master plan, because it is only when one reaches such a level of specificity that it is possible to make apparent the newness of some of the approaches needed for this kind of park, as well as the continuity with the intentions and forms of the nineteenth-century American park movement.

This said, it is important to stress the most critical elements of these new parks; the first one an element belonging to the newness of its form, the second a continuity – albeit one greatly expanded – of a feature of Olmsted urban parks. The first is the matter of connections. As a matter of fact, the only way to make these linear parks succeed lies in stressing their connections along their open-ended linearity. These new parks are basically, intrinsically connective tissue.

The second element is the not always apparent function that these new linear parks have as public promenades. This ties in with the major role given to the promenade in Olmsted parks, which were not quite able to fulfil its possibilities, because of their short span and limited destinations at both ends. Multiply the destinations, give them a panoply of urban, rural, cultural and natural possibilities and this new park becomes a promenade with enormous civic potential.

Diana Balmori is a landscape designer and landscape historian. Founder of Balmori Associates, a landscape and urban design firm which concentrates on public spaces, based in Connecticut, she holds a dual appointment at Yale University.

WILL ALSOP AND RIVERSIDE NORTHAMPTON: THE PRODIGAL RETURNS
Roderick Coyne

Back in the eighteenth century, the millionaire William Beckford was able to realise an extraordinary dream of architecture and landscape for his Fonthill estate in Wiltshire. Now approaching the twenty-first century, the architect William Alsop, who possesses neither a private fortune nor an estate, is planning to transform a stretch of riverside in his home town of Northampton, into what is termed an 'ecological park'. These days, such dreams have to be processed through a variety of public screens and channels, before there can be any hope of realisation. However, the advent of the National Lottery has reintroduced into the culture the possibility of attaining the degree of power over events that privileged figures like Beckford once enjoyed.

We are all natives of somewhere, with a disposition to return either figuratively or literally. An artist returning to his formative landscape would obsessively represent it in some medium or other, but an architect is in the singular, if not necessarily enviable, position of being able to transform it physically. The architect's vision is not kept discreetly to one side for the visitor to refer to or not, but actually intervenes with the landscape itself, removing what was there before and replacing it with something new.

The story of Will Alsop's return to Northampton began with an invitation to give a talk in the town's annual lecture series. His chosen theme was how the disused industrial area to the south of the town centre might be revitalised. The invitation to talk was subsequently converted into an invitation to act, and a scheme began to replace the redundant industrial quarter with an extended cultural and recreational garden.

The spectacle of derelict buildings implicitly seems to ask, not only the forward-looking question, 'What ought to be done with this site now?', but also the more intriguing question 'What was here before?'. An answer to the first question might be better constructed if informed by an answer to the second. The imagined history of a landscape would seem to exercise some sort of rhetorical influence over how it is currently perceived.

FROM ABOVE: Site overview; plan; riverscape; pastoral with horses

Owing to problems with planning permission, the prospective site for the project was subsequently reoriented. The new site occupies a mile-long strip of riverside meadow connecting the old town centre with a new business park in the east, with the industrial decay of the original location now forming merely a questioning backdrop. This second site was a dramatically different prospect from the first, for rather than addressing the recovery of an industrial landscape, it would now be the development of a landscape which was not perceived to be a problem in the first place. The proposition was how an area, already functioning as an informal park, could receive the solution to the problem of the original site.

Exploring this site, walking along the river from the town towards the east, one first passes through a short stretch of public garden and then an open recreational area before this conventional urban park gives way to an extended sequence of meadows and copses, which after a mile terminates abruptly at the A45 road bridge. Bisected laterally by the meandering River Nene, the landscape is also bisected diagonally by a procession of pylons leading from the adjacent generating station. The canopy of power cables, together with the terrestrial boundaries made by a railway line, roads, used and disused factories, not to mention the town centre itself, all conspire to effect a very unpromising prospect. However, within this bleak urban embrace, lies a surprisingly rural world. But because this world cannot break through to the surrounding country-side, it nevertheless remains oddly compromised.

It is interesting to compare an urban park marooned within a town, with a landscape park marooned within agricultural countryside. The abrupt change from urban fabric to the natural fabric of the park, establishes a frame around the scenery that would seem to translate its features into tokens of nature, with nature itself lying elsewhere, whereas the country park, in spite of the wall that often encloses it, is not perceived to be different in its fabric to the landscape beyond. It is simply organised according to different criteria.

The picture to which these frames ultimately refer is the received arcadia as represented by artists such as Gaspar and Claude and as re-presented with pick and shovel by the English landscape designers of the eighteenth century. Even when walking through a hybrid landscape like the site at Northampton, one is nudged into recognition of this picture by encountering some of the key components of the arcadian formula; flowing and still water, mature trees and their reflections, bridges, grazing animals and the inevitable ruined buildings.

The concept of parkland is intimately tied to that of painting, and unlike a photograph, nothing unintended is included. There are no shades of grey between the primary components. The hold that this edited view of nature has on our imaginations, is possibly derived from the basic paintings that we make as children; a house surrounded by grass and framed by a tree and a pond. The home is the focus of a child's life just as the building is the focus of a painting by Claude.

Besides the shattered hulk of the power station that looms over the south bank of the river, the only other building that currently interrupts the landscape, is what is apparently a fragment of the changing rooms of a now vanished open-air swimming pool. This feature forms the main point of contact between the present landscape and the personal landscape of the architect's childhood, and also between the proposed scheme and the area's history. For one component of the plan is the reinstatement of the swimming pool – albeit an indoor one – adjacent to the site of the original. All that can be discerned now is a shallow depression in the meadow obeying the pool's original contour. No one seems to know exactly what caused its demise, although it must have been something more abrupt than the proverbial 'fall of dust' that has overwhelmed countless historical remains.

The impression that nothing has changed is as disconcerting as the impression that everything has changed. We tend to have a fascination with things and places that seem to remain the same. The reason is probably due to our irrepressible longing to cheat mortality; if a place seems not to have changed, then perhaps we haven't either. But a missing swimming pool reminds us that the clock ticks on as expected.

The scheme, which Alsop terms 'not a park and not a street' – with respect to how it will connect the old town centre to the new business park – will be a sequence of cultural and recreational venues following the course of the river. As well as giving shape to the landscape, the river also divides it, and the scheme's most significant contribution will be the uniting of the two embankments in the form of a suite of bridges, all possessing a different ulterior purpose.

Interposed between these, on both embankments, are a dozen or so 'strips', again each with a different function and name. There are also features which neither bridge the river nor embank it, but actually float on it. These are entitled 'floating boxes of delight', inheriting their name and certain characteristics from an earlier, now defunct, project for the French city of Nantes. This component of the scheme could perhaps be promoted metonymically to address the entire project and so implicitly align it with the Chinese 'garden of delight'. This token association is underlined by the ubiquitous use of poetic names throughout the scheme. A glance at the history of Chinese gardens reveals features with names such as, 'place for listening to the sighing pines', 'elevation for remote thought', 'sea observing rock', and 'garden for observing the moon'. Such names were clearly intended to awaken the imagination when using the garden, rather than merely providing a geographical nomenclature. Alsop is also articulating his garden with a similar vocabulary. Currently, the plan of the project is punctuated with

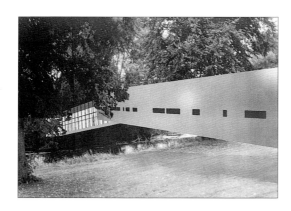

names such as, 'strip of structures for unknown ball games', 'strip of absorption', 'garden of the world' and just to underline the fascination with such names, even a 'bridge of names'.

Building on an unbuilt, and therefore largely unnamed territory, carries with it the proprietorial privilege of being able to name a place that previously was nameless. Builders are in the position of being able to arbitrarily establish and name co-ordinates for our lives. Naming an artwork identifies an object of study; naming a building or landscape feature designates a geographical space that we might actually physically inhabit and so by association become temporarily named also. Calling a building 'the living bridge', even if it bridges absolutely nothing, automatically involves the visitor in the metaphoric relationship between the two terms. A name certainly has the capacity to condition our response to an artwork or place and this is very much to the point here.

Returning to the Chinese connection, Christopher Thacker in his book on the history of gardens, describes the 'garden of delight' and the earlier 'garden of the unsuccessful politician' as having: '. . . pavilions, bridges, rocky viewing places and shelters set around the shores of an irregular lake. The visitor would proceed thoughtfully, observantly, from spot to spot, composing poems, meditating, pausing to admire the chrysanthemums, to rest with a companion, paint a picture, watch the moon or just drink wine.' Such a description identifies these gardens, like their eighteenth-century English counterparts, as being places for reverie rather than merely for physical exercise. The reverie encouraged by the designers of these gardens, was intended to be refracted through a particular educational prologue, without which many of the allusions would have been lost. However, no such requirement will be necessary when experiencing Alsop's twenty-first-century garden. The reverie induced by looking at water

and the reflective state inspired by analogy with the reflective quality of water, would seem to be an explanation for the common practice of placing cultural venues on embankments. What is uncommon, however, is the idea of placing such buildings on structures that actually bridge the water.

The experience of being neither here nor there, with respect to water, appears to temporarily suspend any normal frames of reference. Acknowledgement of this phenomenon would seem to make the idea of placing a facility such as an art gallery, mid-stream, rather an appropriate one. The suite of bridges, which began their life as a series of paintings, all have an ulterior purpose, and as such, will join a very select club of structures. Bridges at Bath, Florence and Venice all support shops, and the Château Chemonceau extends itself across the Loire, but apart from these, no other contemporary examples come to mind. A famous historical example, is of course the old London bridge, which besides shops, even had its own church. (Incidently, just down the river from the site of this bridge, Will Alsop may well be building London's second inhabited bridge at Blackfriars, in the form of a new arts complex for the ICA.)

The seven bridges at Northampton have been given names that, in large part, are self-explanatory. For example, the 'art bridge' is to house a temporary exhibition space, the 'swimmer's bridge' is to incorporate the aforementioned swimming pool and most interestingly, in the context of the town's history, the 'shoemaker's bridge' is to provide a museum of shoes. In acknowledging the metaphoric value of 'the bridge' in the sense of 'bridging the gap', the water of the River Nene variously stands for the gap in history, the gap in available products, the gap in the forum for art, for example. The river is deliberately set up as a figurative boundary to be bridged.

Other features of the garden are to be provided in the

ABOVE: Art Bridge; CENTRE: Swimmer's Bridge;
BELOW: Shoemaker's Bridge; Bridge of Names

form of strips, separated from one another by low walls or hedges. These are to include such facilities as a library with an Internet terminal, gymnasium, recording studio, restaurant and, leading back into the 'uncultivated' landscape, a shop specialising in picnic provisions.

Such a garden, with its emphasis on utility, clearly has its direct ancestor not in the aesthetic tradition of garden design, but in the Victorian parks and garden schemes which provided the general public with open spaces for recreation and entertainment. Although these gardens borrowed some of their aesthetic appeal from private landscape gardens (more usually the formal elements), they were essentially designed as places for people to go and do things in, rather than to contemplate nature.

Certainly this functional aspect of Alsop's garden will save its architecture from the sad fate of many landscape garden structures, the symbolic purpose of which has been undermined by neglect and graffiti. Many of these buildings took the form of replicas of the contemporary ruinous state of the classical or gothic originals and not their complete form. The irony is that the agents of these evocations have themselves become the victims of decay; the decay of the representation cannot seamlessly run into the representation of decay, not without the message turning back on itself.

At Stourhead, the buildings that are most successful at resisting this fate are those large enough and complete enough to function as 'proper' architecture. The Pantheon, for example, transcended its purely ornamental status by providing a servicable interior space. The viewer, however, was invited specifically to address something that was purely ornamental. The buildings were meant as representations of architecture and not architecture itself. At Northampton, this struggle between ageing form and enduring symbol will be replaced by Alsop by the very contemporary struggle between intrinsic form and efficient utility.

The component of the project where this struggle between form and utility will be least in evidence, will be the Millennium Box, an empty cavernous structure to replace the derelict power station on the south side of the river. The interior will be divided and franchised to a variety of businesses in order to provide ongoing funding for the upkeep of the garden.

Alsop's hungry style and taste for exotic construction belies the sober planner that performs beneath the table-cloth. A bespoke company has been set up especially to enable this complex scheme to flourish. The purpose of this company is to formally involve the services of a specialist to help solve the myriad of political and legal problems that such a unique enterprise necessarily generates.

How this enterprise will affect what is largely a commuter town is difficult to predict. But it is not too far-fetched to suggest that it may provide the public with the incentive to travel in the return direction. Clearly, this proposal is so unusual in principle and particulars, that if realised, it will become something of a tourist attraction, both for its confluence of amenities and for its potential status as an exhibition of contemporary architecture.

Because of the pastoral nature of the site, it is difficult, when reflecting upon the proposal, not to evoke the context of the English landscape garden tradition, however inappropiate to the project this may be. Walking around the site, the viewer encounters a series of visual hints that connect with the familiar parade of Arcadian vistas. However, because of the density and variety of its features, Alsop's proposal resists any slippage into these picture frames. The scheme is only comprehensible in plan; indeed, Alsop's series of paintings – from which the project was generated – are depictions of objects and not representations of prospective views. Currently, the computer screens in Alsop's office are busily realising the various components, but we will have to wait for the garden to be built before we can have any sense of its place in the landscape – and what better justification could there be for realising a three-dimensional idea, than to answer the question, 'What will it look like?'

Roderick Coyne is an artist who works with photographic installations.

PETER LATZ & PARTNER
EMSCHER PARK

Duisburg

The project began in 1990 with an international competition, and in 1994 the first parts of the park were officially opened. There is a clearly evident dialogue between decay and the intentional demolition of old industrial substance, which form the basis of this project. On this site, where smoking chimneys formerly marked the landscape and air pollution covered the grass on the embankments with a metallic film, a large park is being created from the most fantastic images.

Parts of the industrial 'heritage' – huge buildings and halls, ore deposits which look like ancient Egyptian temples, a parking area – were transformed from elements of mass production into working areas of the park.

Rail and road bridges, emptied tunnels, and the extensive underground galleries and manholes allow pedestrians to move through the park, and present interesting possibilities for future development. The park's overall design is deliberately as chaotic as a 'real' landscape, relying on abstract basic elements. Thus, the most significant elements become landscape, despite their original purpose as industrial structures. The remaining pollution has to be carefully treated, and through this process people can be made aware of their industrial heritage in a newly interpreted manner.

Fantasy freely interprets the structures and spaces, regardless of the historic function they may have had: the old walls of the bunker buildings

OPPOSITE: The opening ceremony; ABOVE, L TO R: Blast furnaces; climbing walls

ABOVE: Small amphitheatre; RIGHT: Walls of the bunker buildings open on to enclosed gardens

become 'rock faces' in a mountain landscape, and the rigid tangle of rusty blast furnaces looks like a hunting dragon. The central idea is to adapt the purposes of the structures; the blast furnace becomes an observation tower or the 'Matterhorn', dominating the surroundings. It might seem absurd to compare elements of the park to the Alps, but climbing paths across the masses of concrete – following the cracks, hollows and scars – do give that impression and are used for training by members of a climbing group.

The demolition of the 150-feet-high tower presented another possibility – since it could not be converted, it could instead be recycled into new building material. The tower previously housed

the grinding of coke, coal and mineral ore, providing the inspiration for our contemporary equivalent – to create a blooming landscape, an open area for large gatherings, a small amphitheatre and a boscage of trees – without any horticultural soil.

Red concrete was similarly made from the industrial detritus, and was used to construct the theatre next to the old transformer station. Colours are important throughout the site; red symbolises the earthy, the usable; blue the touchable, especially among the higher levels. The grey and rusty areas mean that these structures cannot be traversed.

The massive walls of the bunker buildings were opened to allow their

Amphitheatre

transformation into walled gardens with climbing plants and herbariums. Here, 'garden' means the occupation of individuals within the existing fabric and learning about the environment and vegetation with the help of intellect and hand. It is an archetypal form of discussion, one of human society with nature. Gardens are resting places, where people can confront large dimensions within a small space. Plants have been brought in from Norway, South Africa, Brazil and Australia which possess the special characteristic of being able to survive in the artificial substrata of ashes and slag heaps.

The park consists of five individual systems, the lowest level of which, the water system, required the most alteration. The site is divided by a deeply-set waste water ditch, the Old Emscher. A concept was developed for the water park of a still-water system fed by rain water. From streets, roofs and squares the rain water is channelled to the water park. Collection and use of the water is visible in every situation, and as far as possible, closed pipes bridge traffic areas.

The spatial design concept intends to use the existing profile of the Old Emscher after the construction of an underground duct for waste water. The profile contains different water zones:
- Planted bank areas (10-50cm).
- Normal zones (50-200cm).
- Deep zones (up to 250cm) for settling.
- Gravel and sand banks.

The central section of the water park is the clear water channel which comprises both shallow and deep water zones together with a settling ditch. The straight line of the embankment is fragmented by different types of vegetation. Water flow is purified before reaching the planted ponds by gravel filters to remove polluting dusts.

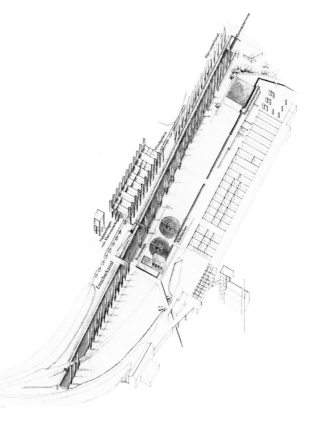

OPPOSITE: Formation of railway lines; ABOVE, L TO R: Pilings; water channel; BELOW, L TO R: Water channel; railway lines

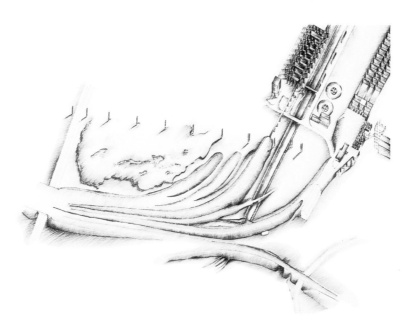

The water channel shows natural processes occurring in an otherwise devastated and unnatural situation, where they take place according to ecological rules, but are initiated and maintained by technological processes.

Straight-lined ribbons and winding loops of railway tracks are spread net-like over the landscape, establishing new relationships with the surroundings. Situated mostly on high dams, they offer the local people a panorama of the urban landscape which was previously denied to them. In the centre, the tracks come together to create a formation of rails that looks like the strings of a harp, and from the highest point of the blast furnace they resemble the stretched-out fingers of an open hand.

A catwalk has already been built on the track of an old elevated railway, on the restored heads of the pilings. In the future, rails will be reintroduced for the running of mobile cafes and service equipment. Essential parts of this foot-bridge are constructed from recycled materials. The 'Piazza Metallica' was created in the open space among the blast furnaces; steel plates, originally used in the process of casting molten metals, were assembled on a bed of sand after being cleaned with compressed air to remove the encrusted ashes.

Only half of the park is completed to date, but it represents a cheerful experiment with nature. This point does not necessarily need to be recognised by visitors to the park, who can freely enjoy the discovery of their own 'nature' within it.

FROM ABOVE: Channelling rain water; creating a landscape; the Piazza Metallica; OPPOSITE: Experimenting with nature

ANDROPOGON ASSOCIATES

Crosby Arboretum

Picayune, Mississippi

The native landscape is the sum of conditions to which indigenous plant and animal communities are adapted. Local plant communities are the essential expression of the place and support the wildlife with which they have co-evolved. In the present global environmental crisis, what we are losing is not simply individual plant species but the complex relationships of plants to other plants, to wildlife and to place. Andropogon Associates, in preparing a plan for Pinecote at the Crosby Arboretum, incorporated natural patterns into the design of the landscape in order to set the stage for nature to re-establish the natural functions which support a rich complexity of species.

The mission of the Crosby Arboretum is to celebrate regional character and to demonstrate the relationship between human culture and the natural landscape. Located within three southern Mississippi counties, the Arboretum now includes a network of natural areas covering 1,700 acres. The purpose of these natural areas is to preserve typical native habitats and to provide sites for long-term ecological research. These sites are considered to be genetic archives and are protected from any development. The site chosen for Pinecote, which was to be the public facility for the larger Crosby Arboretum, was located in the lower Pearl River Basin – the low-lying, sandy landscape of the southern coastal plain, locally called the Piney Woods.

In the design for Pinecote, Andropogon Associates, and the Arboretum Director, Edward Blake, formed the core of the planning team. The Arboretum was named for LO Crosby, founder of the Crosby Lumber Company – his daughter, Lynn Gamill, provided much of the vision and energy which drove the establishment of this unique institution. This plan had to expand the traditional concept of master planning to create a bridge between the site and its interpretive possibilities, between scientific and artistic expertise and between a wide variety of specialists, from horticulturists to cultural anthropologists.

The goal was to create a new synthesis of the artistic values of drama, beauty and expressiveness, with the scientific values of the correct relationships between plant and plant, plant and place. The design was

Before – Pinecote forms the heart of the Crosby Network. The site was originally uniform and undistinguished

During – a programme of pulsed burns of varying intensities was used to foster a rich mosaic of meadow types with the pine savannah

After – a rich tapestry of wild flowers and tall grasses developed between the open groves of longleaf pine

governed by three principles:
- The design would grow out of the inherent qualities of the place – the biome, the region, the local plant communities and habitats, and reflect the cultural history and indigenous architecture of the Piney Woods.
- All design at the Crosby – thematic structure, site organisation, interpretive paths, plant displays, architecture and even site management techniques – would reveal the major natural processes of the Piney Woods and express the evocative qualities of this place.
- Planting design would celebrate native plant communities and reflect the 'architecture of nature' – the underlying structure and organisation (expressed as pattern) of each plant community type.

Pinecote was a discouragingly undistinguished place to develop an arboretum that would display a rich variety of native plant communities and habitats. This 64-acre site previously had a number of agricultural uses, including a Tung oil plantation and strawberry field. The site was initially flat, uniform and undistinguished; the slight but telling differences in topography and the subtle drainage patterns were nearly obliterated by a century of farming. Mapping the potential natural vegetation revealed the possibilities for a diversity of plant habitats. These potential habitats occurred on the site along two continua: a successional gradient, showing the development of plant communities over time; and a moisture gradient, showing the changes in environmental condition, particularly in relation to the depth of the water table. One half of the site had been repeatedly burned, dividing it into burned and unburned areas. The site structure revealed in this initial exploration provided the basis for the site design and for the themes and locations of the four major path loops: the introductory path, which reveals the diversity of the site; the lake path which explores lowland habitats; the long path which contrasts burned and unburned areas; and the forest interior path at the Gum Pond.

In developing the plan, man-made changes accentuated potential diversity and were not drawn from images of other regions. For example, the Piney Woods Lake, although not originally on site, was introduced to make a uniform lowland more dramatic and interesting to the public. However, the pond is neither arbitrary in location nor unnatural in appearance; presentation of the lake evokes a southern, rain-fed swamp with still, shallow, tea-coloured water under a canopy of trees, with a foreground of rushes, sedges and aquatic wildflowers. A small stream flowing from the north, which a farmer or a beaver might have dammed up would take a configuration very similar in shape and character to the lake that was constructed.

Pinecote Pavilion, designed by Jones and Jennings of Fayetteville (Arkansas), was the first building on the site and evokes the structure of a southern pine forest. This open pavilion, designed with the long, hot summer months in mind, is particularly appropriate for evening and morning use. The master plan calls for a series of pavilions throughout the site, each located in the heart of a plant association which it interprets. As many as possible of the proposed pavilions will be open-air and use non-mechanical cooling devices, such as wind-collecting towers.

Native plants are frequently treated

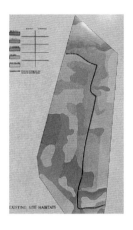

EXISTING SITE HABITATS

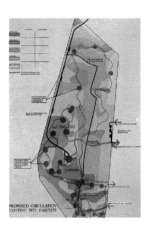

PROPOSED CIRCULATION
EXISTING SITE HABITATS

in traditional horticultural ways and planted in the historical garden geometries of 'bed, bosque, border and *allée*'. Planting at Pinecote is ecological and reflects plant community structure. New plantings are treated as members of a plant community and not as individual specimens. They are displayed in the habitats in which they actually occur, with characteristic companions and in representative organic patterns. Each plant community is described by a local name. A 'buttercup flat', the local term for open lowlands where the yellow pitcher plant proliferates, was created at Pinecote in a location where natural conditions would foster this particular plant community. This species, although abundant in neighbouring wet, open meadows, was poorly developed in the partially drained former strawberry field. A number of different habitat management techniques was used to encourage the spread of this species, including lowering the grade by several inches to increase contact with the water table, reintroduction of the species, periodic burning to expose bare mineral soil (which encourages germination) and removal of competing species.

The use of fire to establish and maintain specific plant communities reinstates a traditional cultural practice in the southern pine woods. With Doctor William Platt, associate professor of botany at Louisiana State University, a programme of pulsed burns of varying intensities was initiated, set at different seasons to foster a rich mosaic of meadow types with the pine savannah. Such management techniques provided opportunities for research into sophisticated habitat management. The aim of the design and management of each exhibit was to transform the latest, best scientific understanding into compelling visual images and every intervention, from educational programmes to vegetation management, was designed to reveal and express the unique qualities of the site.

This project was ambitious and far more difficult than the creation of a traditional arboretum. In a short time, staff were trained, infrastructure and interpretive exhibits put in place, and the country's first ecological arboretum was created from a site considered by many to be without scientific merit or aesthetic interest. In the years since this project began, many talented staff members and visiting experts have contributed to a deeper understanding of this place. The Crosby Arboretum is the first in the Gulf South to preserve, display and interpret the native plant communities of one of the Gulf's major tributaries – the Pearl River Basin. When a place is understood, preserved, repaired and celebrated, it can create a powerful aesthetic. As the landscape has matured and new exhibits have been realised, the promise of the Crosby Arboretum has been fulfilled. The vocabulary of natural patterns and the expression of the character of the indigenous landscape have revealed themselves as infinite sources of form.

OPPOSITE, ABOVE: Piney Woods Lake prior to construction. The proposed lake outline was mowed on the ground, and the board, staff, and scientific advisors were invited to review and comment; the completed lake from the same viewpoint. The lake is designed as a southern swamp with still, dark, shallow water under a canopy of trees with a foreground of rushes, sedges, and aquatic wild flowers; OPPOSITE, CENTRE: View across the lake to the pavilion; boardwalks bring visitors out into the lake through the banded aquatic plantings; OPPOSITE, BELOW: Forest interior path through the Beech Magnolia forest; 'the buttercup meadow', a local term for open lowlands where yellow pitcher plants now proliferate, due to habitat management techniques; FROM ABOVE: Concept design for Piney Woods Lake; plans show the facilities that have been developed since 1980, including Piney Woods Lake, interpretive path journeys, parking access and service roads, Piney Woods Pavilion, and habitat exhibits

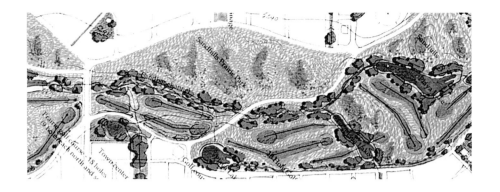

STAPLETON DEVELOPMENT PLAN

Denver, Colorado

Denver's Stapleton Airport closed completely in 1995 when the new International Airport opened. The 4,700-acre site is owned by and entirely within the city of Denver. The Stapleton Redevelopment Foundation, a private, non-profit group, sponsored a plan to create a new community on this land built on sustainable development principles. Located in the high plains prairie, Denver has a semi-arid climate, receiving only 12 inches of precipitation annually.

The plan will integrate environmentally sound practices, such as water conservation, use and restoration of indigenous habitats, and storm-water management using natural drainage. The community will include a mixture of uses – residential neighbourhoods, industrial and commercial areas and the reuse of existing buildings, such as the terminal complex. Runways will be recycled by 'horizontal mining' to convert the old concrete into aggregate for new infrastructure.

Andropogon Associates, as a member of the 'core team' of consultants (*see page 69*), participated in all stages of the planning process, with the particular responsibility for designing a

'natural drainage system' where the restoration of local plant habitats is the basis of the storm-water management and open space systems.

The plan offers an opportunity to restore and resettle derelict urban lands. The central open space of approximately 1,400 acres is the heart of the new community and is the largest single addition to the Denver parks system in fifty years. It symbolises the rebirth of this tract of land as an urban settlement in partnership with natural communities.

The proposed open space integrates various uses, such as golf courses, bike paths, trails and several distinct park types, such as traditional green community parks, active sports centres and natural parks. An extensive storm-water management system using indigenous riparian habitats is the spine of the open space system, and is fully integrated into the recreational facilities.

A natural drainage system uses predominantly open surface channels with natural vegetation, minimising pipes and hard structures. This approach is environmentally sound and more cost effective than conventional engineering solutions. It also provides

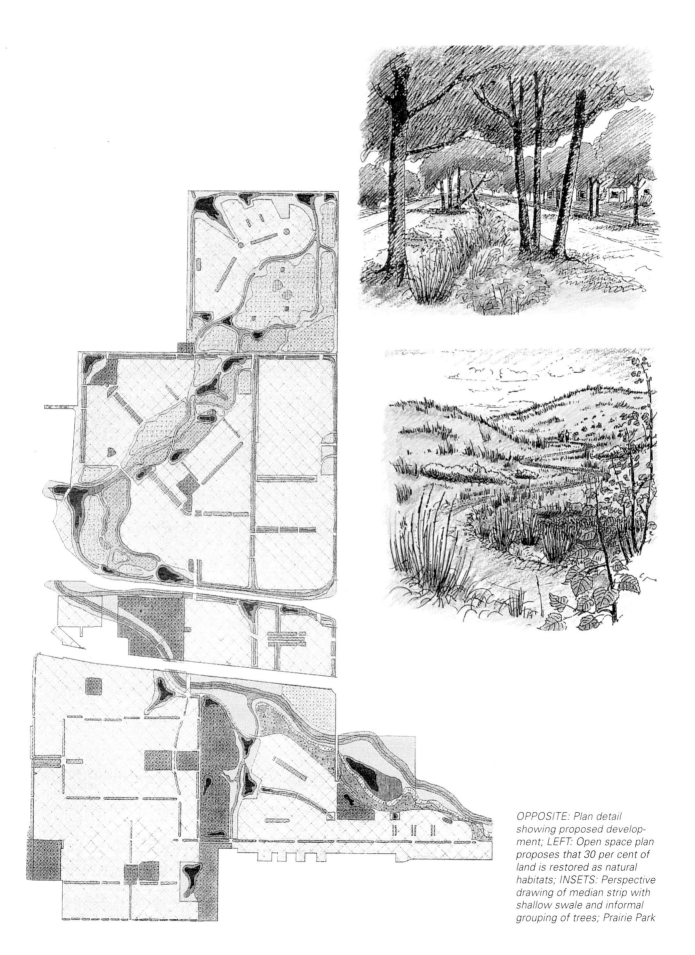

OPPOSITE: Plan detail showing proposed development; LEFT: Open space plan proposes that 30 per cent of land is restored as natural habitats; INSETS: Perspective drawing of median strip with shallow swale and informal grouping of trees; Prairie Park

significant gains in flood storage, infiltration and water quality. The proposed natural drainage network will integrate site drainage and storm-water management into a continuous system of vegetated swales, wetlands and sediments ponds which outfall to regional lake basins. The land area used, while greater than for a piped system, becomes an important recreational and open space amenity for the community as well as providing habitat for native plants and wildlife.

The commitment to sustainability at Stapleton will be most visible in the habitat restorations of the open space system which will celebrate the regional landscapes. The extensive system offers a unique combination of natural habitats, parks and recreational and scenic values. The landscape character of the redevelopment represents one of the most powerful strategies for attracting both people and investors to this site. The goal is to restore and manage the indigenous plant and animal communities of the Western High Plains within a renewed urban fabric. This will be realised at many scales throughout Stapleton, from a regional scale re-establishment of sandhills prairie and restoration of the historic stream channels of Sand and Westerly Creeks, to the smallest re-creations in a garden or schoolyard.

All swales in the main drainage system for Stapleton will be based on the naturally occurring 'sandbar channel' for maximum habitat establishment potential. Natural swales in this arid region are wide and shallow – all Stapleton swales have been given ample width to accommodate the establishment of a similar natural form. During storms, a system of meandering and braided sub-channels with sand bars is created within the body of the main channel. Different plants become rapidly established on the newly deposited mineral soil of the banks and bars forming a rich ribboning of native vegetation including cottonwoods and sandbar willows.

Swales may remain dry for long periods before full development occurs and increases run-off. Such swales would be planted initially with grasses

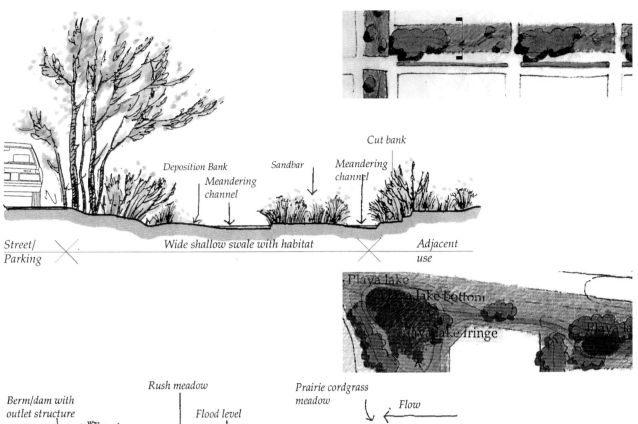

Cut bank

Deposition Bank
Meandering channel

Sandbar

Meandering channel

Street/
Parking

Wide shallow swale with habitat

Adjacent
use

Playa lake
Playa lake bottom
Playa lake fringe
Playa le

Rush meadow

Prairie cordgrass
meadow

Flow

Berm/dam with
outlet structure

Flood level

Groundwater
"Plug"

Groundwater
"Plume"

and other plants suitable for the drier conditions. Some swales might be planted with the extended vocabulary of the 'woody draw' such as the green ash, American elm and box elder.

The 'Playa Lake' is the model habitat for all of the open ponded areas on the site regardless of whether they are for storm-water storage or water quality improvement, although there may be structural differences depending on the specific use and location and maintenance requirements. The Playa Lake is essentially an ephemeral pond that fills with water after storms. Ponds would be designed to empty in a 48-hour period to conform with storm-water detention requirements, however, for habitat purposes, a shallow damp

bottom would be maintained in which a meadow of rushes can be established.

This would be achieved with several techniques used individually or in combination. One method would be to partially impound the ground water plume with a sub-surface barrier as shown. Another would be to supply the pond with a small base flow such as that available from the Montobello drain, or other reuse sources. The basin shape would be a very shallow bowl shape that would allow lake bottom and lake fringe species to vary in their locations depending on ground water availability.

Core Team:
Andropogon Associates, Ltd, Philadelphia PA
BRW, Inc, Denver CO
Civitas, Inc, Denver CO
Cooper Robertson and Partners, New York NY

OPPOSITE: Plan detail showing northern section of Stapleton with re-created sandhills prairie; FROM ABOVE, L TO R: Section of collector swale with smaller meandering channels to restrict flow and create habitat; plan detail of precincts V, VI and VII – north-central section; plan detail of precinct IV showing Playa Lakes; longitudinal section through a Playa Lake showing integration of flood control with wetland habitats

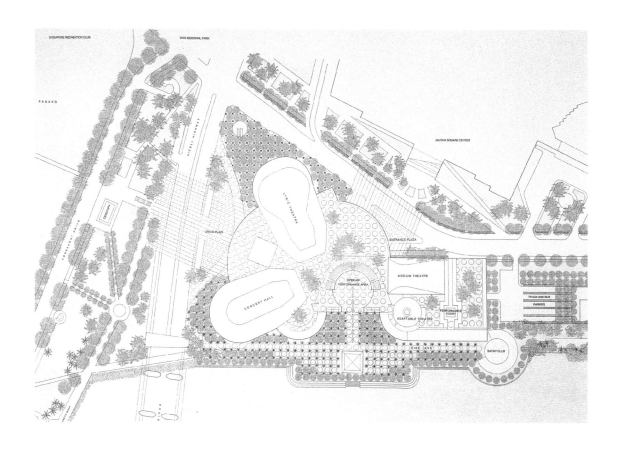

PETER WALKER WILLIAM JOHNSON & PARTNERS
Singapore Arts Center

Singapore's world-class performing Arts Center is scheduled to open in the year 2000. Landscape architects Peter Walker William Johnson & Partners teamed up with architects Michael Wilford and Partners, Ltd (London) and DP Architects PTE, Ltd in Singapore.

The site for the centre is seen by PWWJ as a significant component of a 'green' necklace along the water and city fronts of Singapore. Connecting with the richness of both the historic and contemporary city, this major international cultural centre provides an important image for the convergence of the traditional and the innovative arts of the Asian cultures that find their meeting place in Singapore.

The proposed landscape design for the esplanade is intended to be neither Eastern nor Western, but rather a combination of visual ideas producing a new urban garden unique to Singapore. Rather than a series of discrete gardens, the plan reflects the concept of the landscape as a continuum of the architecture, extending and dramatising the connections of the structures and the flow of the entire space, including both the indoor and outdoor sites. The proposed landscape is composed of a three-dimensional matrix of large circular stone 'coins' which alternate with a high canopy grid of palms and *Polyalthia longifolia*, and a lower flowering understorey of shade producing *Cassia javanica*. The

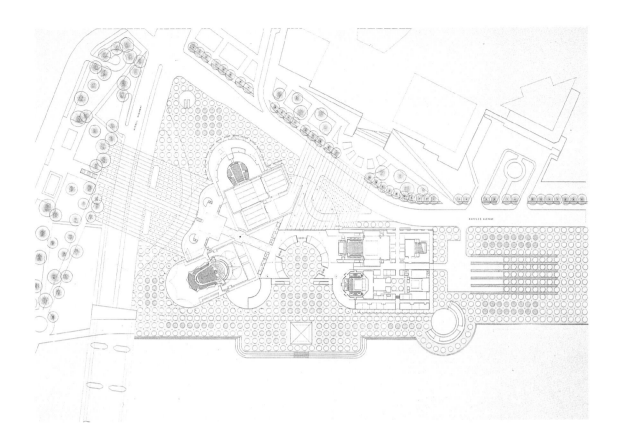

OPPOSITE: Master plan; ABOVE: The esplanade; BELOW: A forest of
stainless steel light wands at the entrance to the Arts Center

vertical scale of the palms and *Polyalthia*
relate to the architecture of the great
glass-skinned performance halls on the
water side, extend the existing green
park along the esplanade, and reach
out toward the existing cricket field
park. In some cases the stone coins
would be elevated to provide seating or
reflecting pools, and elsewhere they are
flush to the ground with an infill
pattern of small granite stone, dry sets.
Fine grasses will be planted between
the stones, and as the many visitors
stroll through the gardens, 'paths' will
be worn into the refined surface while
other areas will be left lush and green.

At the vehicle entrances to the
complex, a forest of stainless steel
wands is proposed at the height of the
underside of the *porte-cochère*. Each
wand would have at its top a small
incandescent light to match exactly the
pattern of lights on the underside of
the canopy.

The stone and grass carpet will also
cover the roofs between the upward
projections of the great halls, providing
a green pedestrian campus between the
various building generated activities.
Programmed and impromptu perform-
ances would spill out of the formal hall
areas into the gardens and promenades,
and on to the roof terraces. Sculpture,
public and performance art are
intended to animate the rich carpet of
the garden, each enhancing the other.

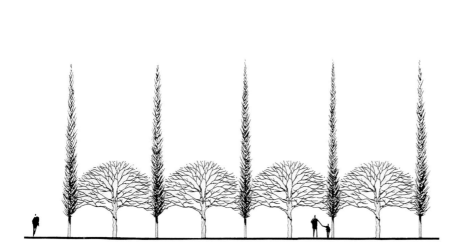

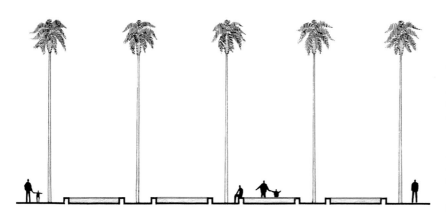

FROM ABOVE, L TO R: Low canopy trees planted in the centre of stone benches filter light and contrast with columnar trees; a row of circular posts replaces a row of stone benches; stone 'coins' are raised as benches. Overhead, the canopy is punctuated by palms; model showing canopy trees planted in stone benches; palms and stone benches; OPPOSITE, FROM ABOVE, L TO R: Stone 'coins' flush with paving; plan showing 'coins' in paving; plan

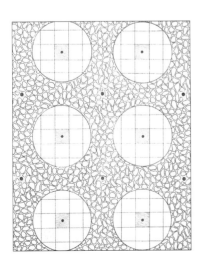

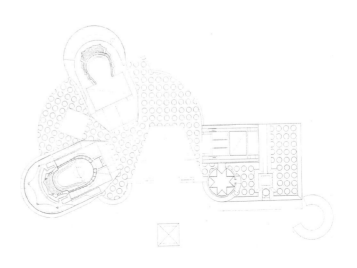

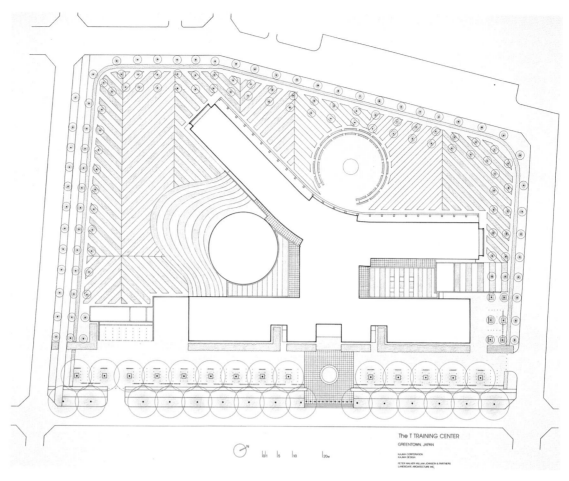

The T TRAINING CENTER
GREENTOWN, JAPAN

KAJIMA CORPORATION
KAJIMA DESIGN

PETER WALKER WILLIAM JOHNSON & PARTNERS
LANDSCAPE ARCHITECTURE INC.

TOKIO MARINE OYAMA TRAINING CENTER

Tochigi Prefecture, Japan

Sited in the northern outskirts of Tokyo, the Tokio Marine Oyama Training Center is located on a generous plot of land in an historically agricultural area. The architectural design by Kunihide Oshinomi of Kajima Design, in collaboration with the garden design of PWWJ, creates a literal oasis that recalls the agricultural past amid the residential and urban landscape of the current city. Formed by two attached buildings which intend to resonate with the predominant element of the land, the plan intimates a spatial dialogue between the refined lines of a main guest room villa and a curvilinear classroom wing, which serves as a metaphor for a barn with its curved form and roof. These structures

provide both a link with cultural history, and a manifestation of a modern architectural concept of simplicity and integrity with the site.

The Walker design demonstrates connections between many of the disciplines and historical threads that have inspired the work. The differentiated sections within the landscape design indicate a direct relationship to a view of agricultural fields from above. As if planted and ploughed with the intentional regularity of farming design, the patterns of this garden offer a familiar aerial image of the purposeful marks of cultivation on the natural landscape. The internal patterns of various 'fields' of the garden, composed of grasses and local gravels, contain

individual and distinct order in striped, zigzag and radiating patterns that reflect both ancient decorative motifs and the contemporary pictorial elements of works by artists like Frank Stella, Alfred Jensen and Jasper Johns, for example. Walker has infused this generalised sequence with a collection of accessible yet mysterious garden components to inhabit the overall pattern and to make the garden liveable as well as viewable. Conceived as a villa garden for the Center, the plan offers a triple *allée* of poplar trees that surround the site, allowing private walkways to separate the centre from the community while still providing glimpses from one to the other.

The arrival courtyard is marked with a large wooden disk of carved timbers lying on a square plane of slate, delineated by a square of light. This bright red sculptural disk reveals a cut-out hole from which emanates a deep violet light. A double curved row of pruned hedges creates an open but protected circular space with a half-hidden pond and concentric ring pool between the hedges and a central fountain. The Tokio Marine Oyama Training Center is a distinguished example of Walker's ability to synthe-sise the conceptual and functional values of a garden, while responding to the strength and poetry of the architec-ture and the unique qualities of the environment. *Leah Levy*

OPPOSITE: Plan; ABOVE: Model showing agricultural villa garden

*FROM ABOVE: Mound covering the
circular wall of the conference room gives
the impression of terraced farm fields;
cross hatch marks of the landscape
undulate over the topography*

FROM ABOVE: Undulating strips of grass and local gravel; inside the 'castle' garden; main 'castle' garden

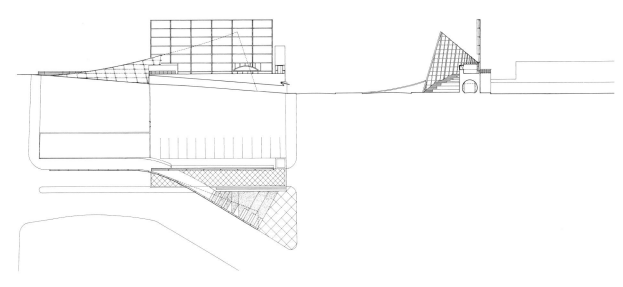

ROGER SHERMAN, CHRISTOPHER DOYLE, ANITA BERRIZBEITIA, HARRISON HIGGINS

DESIGN COMPETITION

Atlanta

Alternate Routes

Public space and urban space, virtual synonyms in historic cities, have diverged in Atlanta. While public space continues to permutate into ever more specific networks of exchange, urban space has atrophied into an unparticularised and uninterrupted space; under, above and in between the lanes of the 'infobahn'. The built public sphere, that intersection of space and information – in which alliances are made, intimacy is fostered and power is both revealed and challenged – risks becoming an extinct phenomenon in the new American city, superseded by the invisible ganglion of economic prerogatives. No longer a destination, it has become the experience of being in between locations.

By intersecting geography and information in a manner that reveals something unexpected about each of them, this project proposes to enrich the experience of the pedestrian, driver and rail passenger's daily voyage.

Drivers turning on to Central Avenue from Decatur Street encounter a tunnel – upon entering, they are spatially transported; continuous video projections animate both sides of the tunnel. The projections create a seamless environment representing an alternate landscape. Each day that landscape changes. On Tuesday one might drive through an alley of laurels in Provence, on Saturday through the sands of the Sahara.

At night the curved plane defining the northbound lanes of Central Avenue and the screen facing the adjacent car park to the west, expand the virtual landscape for pedestrians and drivers alike. Drawn from nature, the projected images along Central Avenue are populated by creatures indigenous to the region, enlarged to monumental scale. The car park wall becomes a celestial theatre with images of alternative weathers and other heavenly occurrences above a virtual landscape, an illusory extension of the real ground of the asphalt lot before it. During the day, the plane and screen thinly define the edges of the spaces adjacent to the project in the manner of a studio backlot.

The pedestrian path between and behind the projection screens addresses not only a difference in the scale of walking and driving, but seeks to enhance the pedestrian's experience

OPPOSITE, FROM ABOVE: Vehicular approach east-bound on Central Avenue, showing curved plane, exit portal from tunnel and rear of car park wall beyond; view south across car park to projection wall at night; ABOVE: Composite drawing showing longitudinal section, transverse section and plan

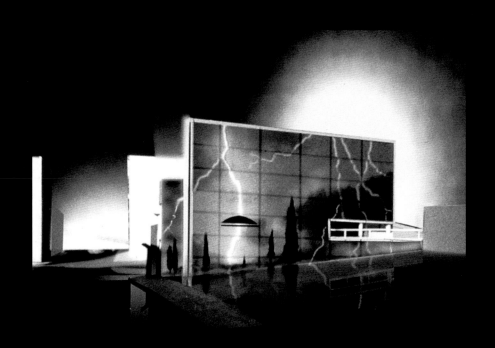

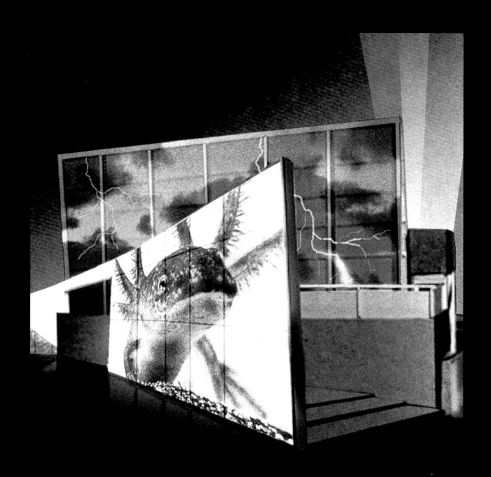

through elements of choice: whether to take an alternative route along Decatur Street and to stop and browse among the Latinate travel booksellers and international newsstand; to have lunch on the steps rising from Decatur Street; or to simply take a shortcut and continue on their way.

Projection spaces seek to make places out of displacement; they make the global local. The pedestrian paths and their accompanying meeting places, on the other hand, are grounded in an intensively local set of conditions and decisions. The space Atlantans pass through on their way to dinner, work, school or MARTA, becomes for a moment a destination in itself. Memories of places outside the city help create memorable places for Atlanta.

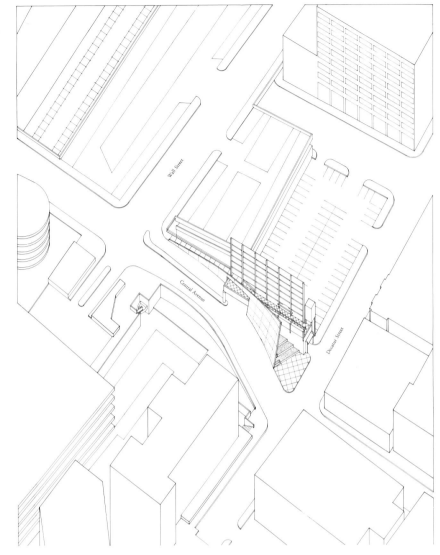

OPPOSITE, FROM ABOVE: Pedestrian paths lead from upper end of Central Avenue alongside curved plane to the newsstand behind car park projection wall; view inside vehicular tunnel westbound up Central Avenue; ABOVE: Axonometric view from southeast; BELOW, L TO R: Site geometry; pedestrian circulation; spatial edges

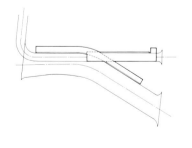  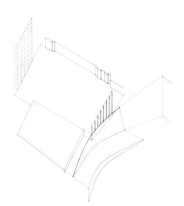

Parking Fields

The new American city of the fax machine, e-mail, and airport terminals is a city of points; numerically identified, autonomous and disconnected from one another. It is a city of destinations without paths. Swarms of parked cars have become one of the most identifiable symptoms of these conditions. They are the dreaded in-between spaces, undifferentiated collections of coordinates at which we leave our cars on the way to indoor sites of exchange. In this project, the neutral grid of the car park is differentiated and enlivened by weaving automobile storage with the other practices of daily life: banking, snacking, buying a newspaper.

One parks in east-west oriented aisles lined by vine-covered metal structures. At four feet in height, these 'hedgerows' establish an artificial horizon at the driver's eye level, replacing that of the landscape, the view to which is blocked by the surrounding retaining walls and stadium. They also line walkways leading to and from each parking space. Each is of a unique design and plant material, and serves as a mnemonic device, or code to help the driver note the specific location of his car in order to more easily find it upon his return. The same is true of the series of covered north-south pedestrian paths which visitors cross. These walkways are alternatively shaded by metal canopies or pollarded trees (sycamore, linden and pear). Specific pedestrian routes are signified by the unique pairing of plant and industrial materials resulting from the crossing of each east-west and north-south pathway. These act together as X and Z coordinates in helping the spectator returning from the stadium seek his vehicle.

Rising from and marking these nodes are 90-feet-high columns which establish a hierarchy of place within the differentiated parking field. Seen as a group from Martin Luther King, Jr Drive and other off-site locations, these columns also constitute a monumental hypostyle porch for the Georgia Dome behind at a scale that is comparable to it. Individually, they function as public spaces would in the historic city, yet here the sun-drenched voids in the traditional urban fabric have taken shape as solids, cool and shaded. At ground level are provided amenities related to spectacles taking place in the Georgia Dome: picnic areas for the inevitable tailgate party, cash machines, electronic ticket dispensers and snack vendors. The columns at the entrance and exit of the parking field contain parking administration and security. Occasionally they also act as a bridge to other off-site destinations as well, for instance, a bridge joins Martin Luther King, Jr Drive at the southernmost column, which provides a stair tower connected to the walkway below.

Clad with fibreglass panels on a steel frame, at night these constructions become projection surfaces. Inside each column a video projector is programmed to move along a specific path, creating images which ascend, spin and disappear from the translucent surfaces both inside and out, while the columns themselves become nearly invisible. During the Olympics, these video figures will be tied to individual sports: monumentally-sized athletes will jump, spin and fly through the night. The installation could similarly be changed to refer to specific events at the Georgia Dome, or to coincide with upcoming events in the city at large. For this reason, each of the columns additionally contains microwave utilities for satellite up- and down-linking for when the parking field is used as an Olympic staging ground.

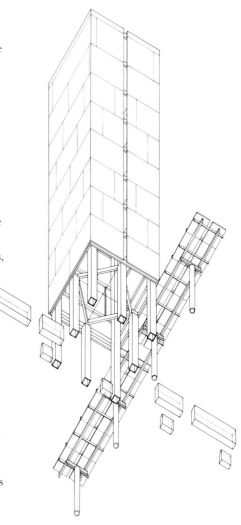

ABOVE: Detail of column/canopy/hedge-row; BELOW: View south from Georgia Dome at ground level, showing hedge-rows and pedestrian canopies with columns above

ABOVE: View north across parking field at night from Martin Luther King, Jr Boulevard to Georgia Dome in the background; BELOW: Axonometric view from north-east

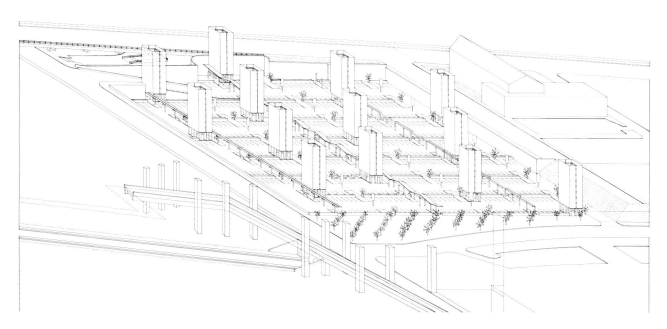

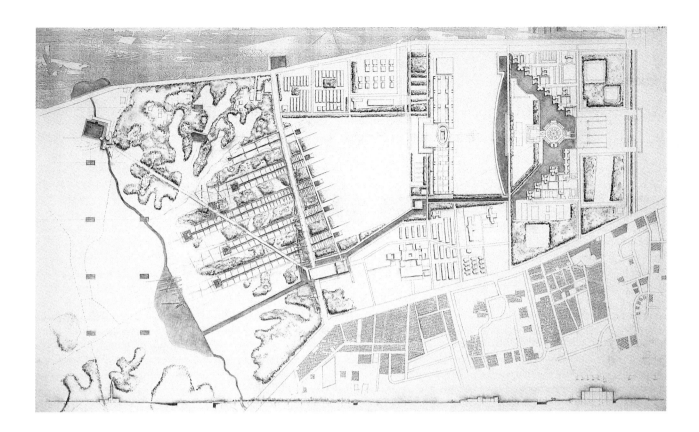

ANURADHA MATHUR

RECOVERING GROUND: THE SHIFTING LANDSCAPE OF DACCA

I am interested in landscapes as flux and change – in cycles of erosion and deposition, construction and destruction, flood and drought, habitation and migration, wetness and dryness. I am interested in landscape not as a static entity that can be defined and contained, but as a shifting, living phenomenon that is both engaging and to be engaged with. Landscape in this active sense is not seen as a commodity or artefact, but as a complex, immeasurable process. To present this distinction is of particular importance to current architectural practice since it is closely linked to the tools that designers and other professionals use in conceptualising and representing landscapes. How we 'see' landscapes inevitably affects how designers intervene in an environment, but also how inhabitants and 'nature' itself play out in time.

A geologist sees wetness and dryness in a landscape as a gradient that transforms soil and affects the resultant structure of topography and vegetation. For a meteorologist, wetness and dryness is measured in the atmosphere and results in changing predictions of weather and precipitation. For occupants of land, wetness and dryness can be felt physically, as one's foot slips off the dry pavement into slush, smelled as the first rain on parched earth or in the acrid depths of a swamp. It may be viewed as reflections and transformations of material, organic and inorganic, besides the patches of mould on damp walls.

OPPOSITE: Recovering ground as the land floods; ABOVE: A public landscape at the edge of the city

Surveying   *Connecting*   *Plotting*

BELOW: Shifting and firm ground – the delta and Louis Kahn

Digging   d   *Cultivating*   e   *Constructing*   f

FROM ABOVE: Flood water gardens and inundated farms; maker of ground – addition/ subtraction, deposition/erasure

People living in extreme conditions of wetness (floods, bogs, torrential downpours) and dryness (deserts), have often constructed their habitation and landscape, in its form and material, to engage and mediate the often life-threatening impact of these two extremes. It is common today, however, to work towards eradicating any discomforting intrusions of wetness or dryness, and by extension of *nature* itself, from at least our immediate environment and if possible a larger landscape. Yet, leaks in dams or domestic piping, wilting geraniums and empty cisterns force us to acknowledge an inherent dependence and accommodation for the processes in a landscape that can be Janus-faced: life-giving and life-threatening.

I am interested in challenging the professional 'viewing' of landscapes from those enclaves of specialisation on the one hand, and the hermetic theoretical discourse on the other, that are so prevalent today. I strive to recover through design inquiry and practice, landscapes that bring together rather than polarise scientific, imaginative and experiential dimensions. This does not necessarily call for an 'inter-disciplinary approach' where the outcome can be described as comprehensive, collaborative, or a compromise. Instead it is a transdisciplinary one, where the act of 'seeing' landscapes in new and alternate ways is constituted through artistic investigation.

Landscape architects often have little tactile engagement with exploring the *real* grounds of their intervention in the process of design. Instead, the site is represented in other mediums – words, numbers, images and, primarily, drawing. How a medium is used depends on and is affected by what landscape design is perceived to be. The making of land-scape requires an engagement with one's ground, be it a drawing, a terrain or a discourse which allows one to explore and reveal – processes *in process*.

Viewing the landscape as a temporal, shifting process and not as an object-ified artefact is central to my intervention in the landscape of Dacca in Bangladesh, a country that sits precariously in the delta of three major river systems – the Ganges, the Bramhaputra and the Meghna. It is prone to cycles of drought and flood, the latter of which, when resisted, often results in vast devastation. Of equal importance to the design challenge posed by ecological extremes is the complexity that characterises the socio-economic context of the people in this region, many of whom live on the 'margin'. These extreme situations further challenge the activity of landscape design as a process of inquiry. My own project is therefore concerned with the 'edge' between built/claimed ground and the shifting/fluxed ground of the flood plain – or the *remaking of ground in a shifting landscape*, physically, socio-economically and metaphorically. It is about addition and subtraction, figure and ground, sedimentation and erasure, in a flat landscape where slight changes in relief are both registered and 'made' by processes of flooding.

The site for the project is the north edge of the Assembly Complex at Dacca, designed by the American architect Louis Kahn, which mediates between the high ground of the city and the low ground of the flood plain. This land once supported extensive farming and scattered dwellings, and was also a back-swamp for the Buriganga River. Over the last few years it has been subjected to *ad hoc* developments, filling and occupation by squatters who maintain a precarious existence in this flood plain. Two decades after it was first conceived as an enclave to the north of the old city, the Assembly Complex is becoming, though still only partially complete, the physical and administrative centre of Dacca. It is under pressure to respond to its new position in the landscape.

In this dynamic delta region, erosion and deposition go on continuously with ebb and flow. The flat topography spreads flood waters evenly, and slight changes in elevation create distinction between inundated and habitable ground. In order to dwell on these dynamics, a device was constructed between high and low areas, which engages in the remaking of ground.

An apparently fragile structure anchored deep in the ground, the 'maker of ground' tenaciously withstands the seasonal flood. It carries the potential of engaging the flood waters and the wind. Its sinewy arms, set in motion by incoming and receding waters and balanced by counterweights, scrapes the silt of the flood plain, slowly yet insistently allowing it to be carried and deposited behind reed barriers, to make new ground.

During a flood almost a third of the country can be inundated, as land and water compete with each other for supremacy. Formerly, people built their houses on mounds to protect them. The ground for these came from the digging of lakes, ponds and canals that also stored water to survive the coming drought. In the last few decades, the pressure of urban growth, compounded by waves of migration from distressed rural areas, has resulted in an indiscriminate filling of the lowlands, primarily at the edge of the city without providing for storage and retention of flood waters. While government authorities are straitjacketed by unimaginative 'sub-division planning' or sporadic 'relief' measures as followups of 'grand plans', the devastation increases as rivers flood.

The design proposal embraces the siting of an agricultural institute between high/stable ground and the low/shifting ground of the flood plain as a continuation of Louis Kahn's Complex. It is an attempt to direct the *reconfiguration* and *reclamation* of this land as a place to 'dwell', in the changing context of Dacca and the phenomena to which it is bound. The site is to be used by the institute for experimental farming of crops that are grown in flood-prone areas as well as for housing immigrant farmers who will be employed to build the infrastructure and manage the farms. The project will be a public park for the people of Dacca: for education, exchange and an evening stroll.

Responding to conditions of flood and drought which requires drainage as well as retention of water, the project is generated by its water structures – the low-lying reservoirs in the flood plain, and the raised reservoirs and canals that define a series of linear gardens and fields connected by paths. The 'fingers' of habitable high ground balanced with low grounds contain these gardens and fields (for experimental farming) which accommodate different levels of inundation. The raised canals and reservoirs store flood waters for the dry season to counter drought. The reservoirs, which are also places for introspection and reflection, terminate the canals and 'continue' the sense of a larger landscape.

The 'maker of ground' is transferred to the canals that traverse the fields of experimental farming, scraping its floor as the flood moves in, keeping the canals free of siltation. As the only verticals in this vast open horizon they become the gateway and the guardians of this city.

HARGREAVES ASSOCIATES
Parque do Tejo e Trancão

Parque do Tejo e Trancão is an 80-hectare urban/environmental park for EXPO '98 in Lisbon Portugal. It synthesises human activity, technological infrastructure (landfill, waste water treatment plant, freeway bridge) and environmental issues by programmatically reclaiming the existing polluted industrial waterfront and turning it into a public amenity and environmental resource. The park generates its formal expression from current and historical hydrological and geological events which occur at the confluence of the Tejo and Trancão Rivers. The park will become a recreational and ecological asset for the exhibition grounds.

A complex agenda was required for this project, including land reclamation, integration of the sewage and solid waste facilities, connection of the park grounds to the local community and the city of Lisbon as a whole, and the development of cultural activities and environmental education with reference to the EXPO '98 theme of the oceans. Additionally, the new park will be a means to increase property values for the urban redevelopment area (160 hectares) proposed at the south-western boundary of the site.

The 80 hectares of abused land allocated for the park is currently covered by three metres of rubble from construction activities and is home to a sewage treatment plant, largest of the three which serve Lisbon. The public cannot help but see this place as a wasted, chaotic and dirty landscape, a perception that needs to be changed in order to market successfully the proposed redevelopment area.

The design envisions spaces and activities of human recreation in a feedback relationship with the technological/ecological processes of re-creation of land and water. People constantly remake themselves and the landscape through play or sport, and through renewed awareness of the environment and its processes of reconstruction. Leisure activities such as biking, fishing, walking, playing, sitting, viewing; and competitive sports such as football, rugby, volleyball, tennis, golf and horseback riding, are engaged in concert with a programme of environmental education. This relationship may enhance and change perceptions or attitudes about waste and unsustainable patterns of re-creation as well. For instance, the

OPPOSITE: Clay model of site; OVERLEAF, FROM ABOVE, L TO R: The central lagoon is a retention pond, storing reclaimed water for park irrigation and creating wetland habitat; playing fields, marshes and piers; playing fields along central pedestrian walk; golf centre; equestrian centre is served by bridle paths which wind among abstract dendritic land forms; Trancão Village

existing primary and secondary systems of sewage treatment will be integrated with a tertiary treatment system based on biological processes of sludge digestion, solar de-watering and wetland filtration. This system will recycle waste water and make it available as a sustainable source for irrigation. Thus the proposed sports fields and the golf course will not only perform the humanistic role of providing opportunities for recreation, but also the more holistic one of ground water recharge.

The joint re-use and manipulation of the landfill and of 575,000 cubic metres of salvaged clay sediments afford new topographical possibilities in the existing, relatively flat landscape. These land forms become key elements in the differentiation of a variety of spaces and functions. The berms are aerodynamically shaped to create pockets of wind shadow in the valleys, which are sheltered play meadows with ridges for viewing and seating. The land forms also play in tune with other systems to create a hydrological network capable of supporting both human recreation and the re-creation of clean water, wetlands and wildlife.

Surface drainage is collected from paths and fields, then channelled in open swales through ridges and valleys across the park and eventually discharged into the V-shaped inlets cut at the edge of the river. There are places atop the landfill itself, where the earth is sculpted into cones containing vents for the methane gas originating from the decomposition of waste taking place underground. They become physical reminders of the elements below as well as orientation markers for the golfers above. Remaking this polluted landscape into a healthy public amenity included the creation of an ecological restoration plan for marshes, wetlands and wildlife habitats, resuming their historic and ecological significance to the region.

In the area immediately west of the sewage treatment plant, canals are sculpted into land forms and woven through the existing waste water infrastructure, drawing attention to its purpose as both a waste water tertiary treatment system and as a wildlife habitat. Sludge drying beds at the berms' ridge line utilise the sun's rays while excess water is filtered out by gravity along the slopes. After this de-watering process, the sludge is harvested and used as both soil conditioner and fertiliser for the park and for demonstration farming and community gardens. The reclaimed water collected by gravity at the bottom of the slopes receives further purification by filtration through wetland plants. These plants assimilate metal, salt and nitrogen, and move gases to the root zone, further sustaining the process of aerobic decomposition.

To mitigate problems of odour in the proximity of the sewage treatment plant and to increase temperature control which enhances the productivity of the facility, an aerodynamic glass and fabric tension structure is proposed to cover the existing primary and secondary treatment facility. Resembling a huge butterfly wing, this structure is meant to draw the attention of curious people to the facility, rather than exclude the process from sight in an inconspicuous structure. In this instance, methane gas is produced as a by-product and could in the future be converted into energy to run the waste treatment plant and to make possible the lighting of the park and evening use of the sport facilities.

The design for Parque do Tejo e Trancão provides exposure to, and a psychological intimacy with, the recycling of waste, the depuration of water and the restoration of wetland and wildlife habitats. The design also envisions spaces and activities of human recreation in a feedback relationship with the technological/

ecological processes of re-creation of land and water. For example, piers provide points of environmental interpretation which inform visitors of the fragile but incredibly rich wetland environment.

The environmental education centre provides the park's visitors with the opportunity to learn about wetland functions, within a philosophy which recognises the importance of integrating seemingly disparate elements such as landfill, waste water treatment and natural ecological systems, by demonstrating that these potential rivals cannot only coexist but can be transformed into valuable places in the landscape, weaving together the infrastructure, wildlife, recreation and education demands of the local region and inhabitants.

Hargreaves Associates has not perpetuated the illusion that subtle corrections can guide us to a good life in harmony with 'conserved' nature or cosy re-created landscapes of the past. A feedback process has been established in the park and many by-products are recycled in the environment as raw materials for a new biomass. The recycling strategy doesn't address only *human* reuse and *human* re-creation, but integrates economical, biological and human systems to create a regenerative method of interaction with the land. People are invited into a landscape that returns to the land rather than subtracting from it. They are drawn in without being threatened, and can enjoy, participate and recreate in the process of learning. The park thus acts as a model for broader systems of production and consumption of resources, which have to change their structural and functional design in order to become sustainable and restorative. By challenging a direct involvement with issues concerning waste, this remade landfill may eventually disclose new solutions for a more sustainable future.

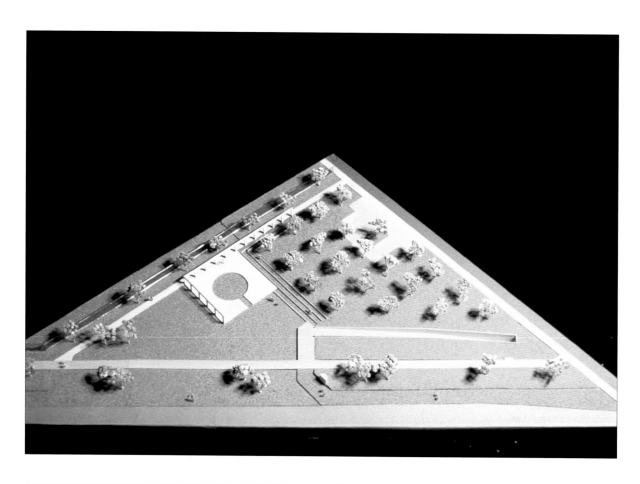

94

M PAUL FRIEDBERG & PARTNERS
PROBING THE FOURTH DIMENSION

The more we depend on sophisticated technology, the more we distance ourselves from contact and understanding of our natural environment. Technology has reduced our dependence on the need to navigate by stars, read weather by wind and clouds, and provide warmth through fireplaces. The technological benefits ease our ability to subsist. However, there is a commensurate loss of experience and loss of connection to the natural environment including the pleasure of living with and reading basic elements and forces that make up or cohabit our world.

It is certainly possible, even desirable, to exist without the knowledge that the earth rotates on a tilted axis around the sun in a predictable course. However, it is not the implication that we have an obligation, moral or functional, to be knowledgeable about the natural environment. Rather, we preserve or facilitate the opportunity and ability to maintain this contact and access to our natural environment. Preserve it for those who are interested, inquisitive, and employ this contact as a source of pleasure. Those who wish to have a

connection with the interrelationship of the environment that sustains us – a direct, not surrogate, contact.

Although light, wind, sun, shadow, reflection, temperature, seasons and time are omnipresent, they are common, familiar and go unnoticed. Yet, their product is change – ephemeral. We who alter the environment through development, mass, or spatial changes require permanent evidence of our efforts and rarely employ these ephemeral effects to enrich our work through temporary alterations, character, or additional layers of information.

Only recently, after what is almost a lifetime of designing the landscape, have I come to realise the opportunities and possibilities of this palette that I call the 'fourth dimension'. The ephemeral landscape – connecting the sensual with intellectual experiences, inner and outer space.

We were recently commissioned to design the following two projects in which existing sites were to be reused for recreational purposes, thereby providing the opportunity to explore and employ some aspects of the unseen yet present fourth dimension.

OPPOSITE, FROM ABOVE: Phoenix Canal project, model of Dottie Gilbert Plaza; model of Yerba Buena Gardens; ABOVE: Arizona Canal project, Hohocum Indians' canal system 2,000 years ago

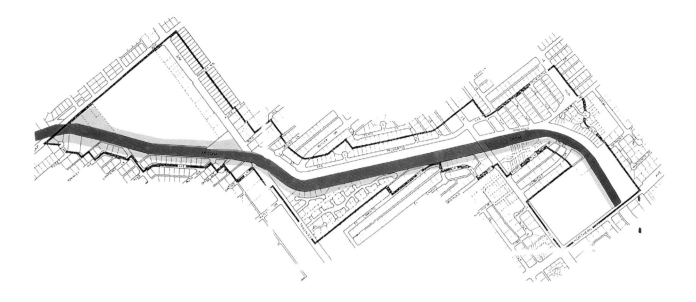

ARIZONA CANAL PROJECT

There are times when it is more prudent to allow things to happen – rather than to make them happen. We came to the Arizona Canal armed with preconceptions, and years of experience, in the process of intervention – only to be disarmed by the canal itself. We, individually and collectively, came to the conclusion that our role is to limit intervention and to illuminate what exists with subtlety and nuance, that any significant intervention – design – would be inappropriate, costly and potentially destructive. Our quest became a search for the soul of the Arizona Canal.

The project confronts us with two forms of development, both premeditated, yet following different imperatives. The canal, created to control and direct melted snow from the mountains as it traverses the desert, follows the discipline of topography and geology. The urban communities, geometric in organisation, are a product of economic determinants. At the point in which these intersect, curious and potentially interesting events occur.

The water, although limited in size, is the dominant experience. It gives life to the environment, it is expressive, has mood, colour and is almost alive. The banks contain and support the water and provide a platform to experience the water. Our concept is to release and reveal the magic inherent in this powerful, yet seemingly simple composition. Our goal was to heal wounds; provide comfort; retain the desert and reveal the beauty of this place by overlaying information that enriches the experience of being in the last vestige of desert in Phoenix.

The intervention sought to express the experience of the linear composition by bringing the visitor closer to the water by lowering the edge of the bank of the canal to the minimum point of functional acceptance and separating cyclists from pedestrian activities. The ground plane was left as barren earth. However, special rooms were invented in which we sought symbolic, metaphorical and historical references of this place. The device of 'rooms' allowed the visitor to step out of the canal into a special place with a distinctive message about the environment.

The water room employed a natural and manageable process of climate control through shade and evaporation

Canal plan

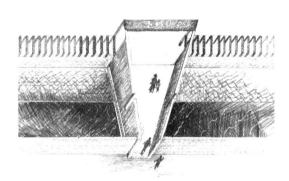

by borrowing water from the canal for visual, spatial, and climatic experience.

All rooms accomplish similar objectives with subtle adjustments or additions to the land forms, contours and planting, in conjunction with a simple palette and vocabulary of materials for structures and pavements – all characteristics of the Arizona desert climate. For example, each room sought to:

- Illuminate the meaning of the Arizona sun and sky.
- Identify place in relation to specific times of the day, and season.
- Bring the botanical and biological environment into focus.
- Express the specifics of the unique place and region.

- Reveal the beauty in the currents, reflections, and moods of water.
- Reflect on past history.

Our approach did not involve innovative elements, but innovative concepts; an holistic approach through the fusing and integration of art with the landscape. We sought to bring the visitor into closer contact with their environment to make it more accessible. A tree is shade, leaf structure, silhouette, shadow pattern, fruit, bark, micro climate, flower. A wall is bench, line, pattern, shadow line. A tower is marker, cooling device, reflection of an historic form, vantage point to a specific orientation, place. An overlook is a place to fish, to see the sunset, the reflections on the water, to view the birds. The didactic is no imperative – no 'must do', or 'must see'. The level or manner of encounter with the environment is strictly discretionary. We see a design that is reduced to the essence of a single unified form – this is the rejection of an aggregation of elements, the rejection of visible design. The task was to illuminate the beauty of what is already there: the canal, desert, the sun, sky and trees.

FROM L TO R, ABOVE: Water rooms; CENTRE: Sundial; water table; BELOW: Bridge; room with a view

YERBA BUENA GARDENS PROJECT

This project conversely suggests a total transformation of place, that of transforming a hostile, vacant, barren, windswept rooftop into a compelling, unique public garden.

Although primarily addressing the unfulfilled curiosity and limitless imagination of children, this place serves all; young and old, community and city. The challenge was to use traditional elements of landscape design to tap the creative energy of children. The controlling formal composition is wrought out of the concept of a single common circulation system for able and disabled alike.

To accomplish this, and respond to the two-level system required walls and bridges. The walls are clad with slate,

enabling and encouraging children to express themselves by the opportunity to draw on them, to create murals and games, to use the wall creatively and to provide, with changing graphics, a kinetic overlay to the space. The slate pattern is calibrated into feet and metres defining and communicating vertical measurement and distances. The handrails of the bridges are designed as sound tubes through which the children can communicate with each other.

The central fountain is activated by movement sensors. Playful activity orchestrates the water display. A play stream originating from the fountain allows for manipulation of the water as gravity carries it downhill. Windmills

FROM ABOVE, L TO R:
Problem solving mural;
player wheel; experimental
sand play; sun cannon;
cognitive game mural;
xylophone/periscope

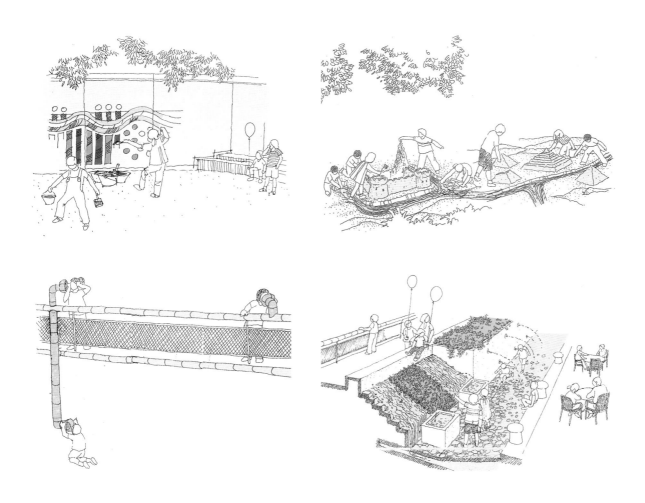

generate electricity for special lighting; the sand area is furnished with special water features providing opportunities for sand castings, surface patterning and scientific experiments.

Additive elements such as telescopes, sun cannons, periscopes, listening vessels (by artist Douglas Hollis) and more, provide playful experiences that bring the child into contact with the invisible components of the environment and the phenomena of environmental physics without appearing didactic.

In the Sundial garden we provided the foundation for changing events such as art installations or the construction of small structures for fairs and bazaars. The playcircle was created as a special playground equipped with creative construction materials stored within the area, which provides the children with the opportunity to have a physical impact on their environment, in the spirit of the adventure playground. Low retaining walls double as play trails, with animal foot or claw prints embossed in the pavement.

Yerba Buena Gardens and the Arizona Canal System are the tip of the iceberg of creative possibilities discovered by tapping the potential of the fourth dimension. It is a new frontier with unlimited borders.

FROM ABOVE, L TO R:
Drawing wall; sandcastle;
sound tube; water play

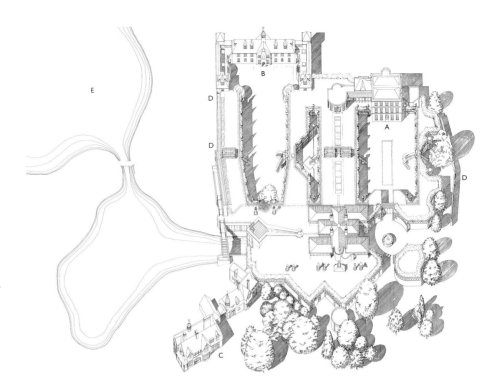

EDWARD CULLINAN
ARCHITECTS
RMC

The simple garden is a composition of offices, social facilities, sports facilities, laboratory, training school and residential accommodation in new buildings which lie between three old houses and two listed garden walls. The new buildings are used to create landscaped garden settings for the three old buildings. They respect the old buildings by creating a place for them, rather than the more common approach of half-copying their styles.

The three old buildings are Eastley End House (*see A above*), an early eighteenth-century Palladian manor house, Meadlake House, its early nineteenth-century stable block (*B*) and the Grange, an asymmetrical late nineteenth-century house, red brick and half-timbered in the Thames Valley Tudor style (*C*). These are integrated with the garden walls which complete the site boundary (*D*), and which are themselves an extension of the red brick walls which run along both sides of the roads through the neighbouring village of Thorpe. Outside the buildings and the boundary walls to the north and east, lie large lakes which result from gravel extraction (*E*). These lakes are bordered by Thorpe Park, which started as semi-cultural, with scaled replicas of all the world's tallest buildings; for example, Mississippi steamboats, Robinson Crusoe's Island and a farm which contains historic breeds, but recently it has become more 'fun fair' in its nature, with scary rides and cable water skiing. South-east of Thorpe Park and the village is the junction between the M3 and the M25 London orbital motorway, and it is these connections and proximities which make the site a desirable commercial location.

A view from the east shows the Grange and the boundary wall across an inlet from one of the lakes. A second view shows the boundary wall seamlessly connected to the extended flank of Meadlake House; and a third view shows a critical break in the western flank wall where one is invited to enter the world of the landscaped gardens within. These are the gardens which create the necessary new accommodation but also make settings for the old buildings. First one arrives in an entrance court, then proceeds to a second court which uses offices to make a setting for Eastley End House.

Planometric

This leads into a small white court designed to bounce light into offices, and to a court which is made to contain the north facade of Meadlake House. To these four external courts is added a fifth internal court or foyer, surrounded by sports facilities and restaurant, topped by dining rooms and containing a swimming pool. This is the essential courtyard from which the location of all parts of the complex can be understood and where one finds the front doors to the extensive offices, training school and laboratories – truly a place of reception.

The whole is referred to here as a simple garden because, in the great garden tradition, it consists only of the semi-formal part of the landscape which lies close to the mansion, within the surrounding walls as distinct from the great informal landscape of Thorpe Park and beyond which lies outside those walls.

FROM ABOVE: Eastley End House; view from the east, showing the Grange; the entrance court

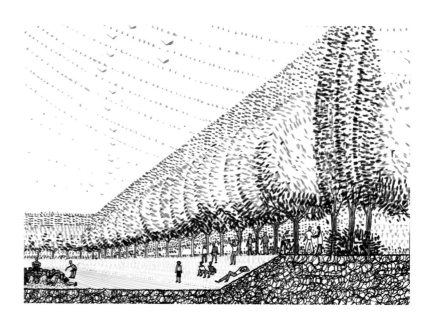

MASTER PLAN FOR THE UNIVERSITY OF NORTH CAROLINA AT CHARLOTTE

In addition to the Carol and Irwin Belk Track and Field Center, five more large playing fields are needed by the university for its 25,000 students. All these courts and fields require tree belts to reduce wind and to provide shade. These tree belts also go far towards reducing the obtrusiveness of the lighting systems needed by most areas.

The playing fields are considered a major contribution to the balance between softscape and civic spaces on the university campus. With the substantial improvement of the surrounding of many existing fields, and with the careful addition of many more as an integrated part of the landscape scheme, the master plan approaches completion.

Great value is placed on the inclusion of a large lake in the valley of Toby Creek, which would bring considerable benefits to the university. Options for the lake include a series of integrated terraces – providing a richly varied area of landscaped water gardens which could be used for recreation and research – and a natural water meadow, an open area for passive recreational use, which could accommodate various degrees of wetland restoration.

The lake would provide a significant feature in the landscape of the university, which would look particularly impressive when viewed along the length of the lake. It could be used for sporting events, such as canoeing, rowing and rafting, and might contribute significantly to controlling surface water run-off, which will increase as the university grows. It could be designed in a way to complement both the formal and found landscape as shown on the complete master plan. In addition, excavated matter from the lake bed might be used to landscape the quarry north-east of Mallard Creek Church Road, or to turn it into a golf course.

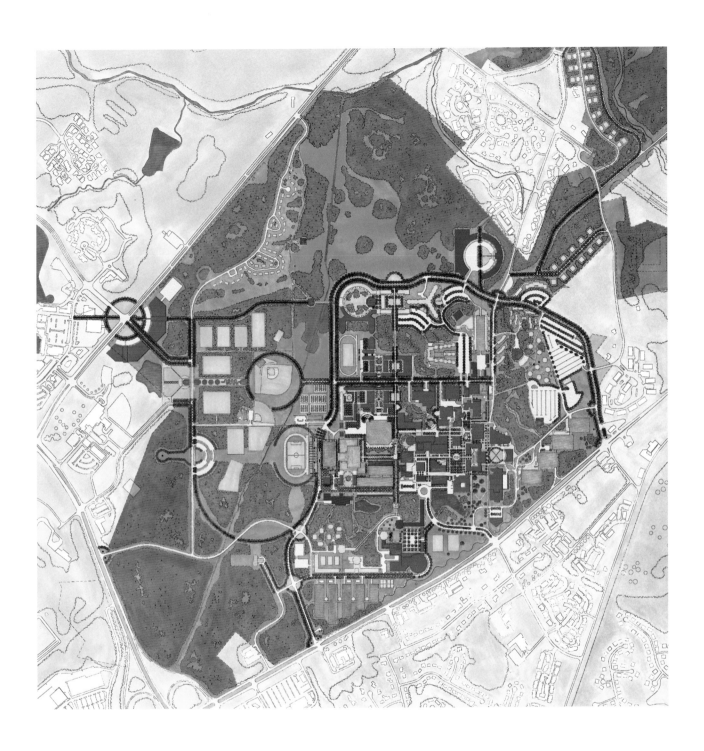

OPPOSITE: Sheltered rugby fields;
ABOVE: Playing fields

Lake options

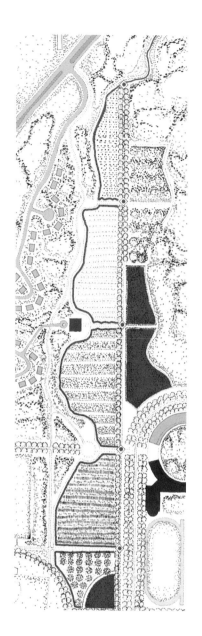
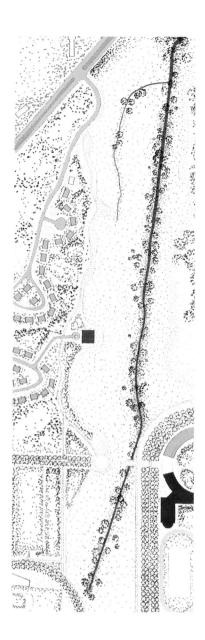

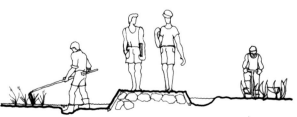

Complete master plan

SIR GEOFFREY JELLICOE, JOHN AND VALERIE WINTER
WALSALL CIVIC CENTRE

In early 1995, Sir Geoffrey Jellicoe and John and Valerie Winter jointly entered a landscape design competition for Walsall Civic Centre. For Jellicoe, this was a return to a town where he had been commissioned to undertake a garden project some thirty years earlier; a Memorial Garden close to St Matthew's Church in the centre of Walsall. Today it stands resplendent and well-tended, a much-loved sanctuary for the citizens of a busy and prosperous Midlands town. Jellicoe and the Winters did not win the competition. However, the project submitted is no less admirable, and important in that it is the last Jellicoe scheme of any scale (or so Jellicoe advises). John and Valerie Winter, as architect and landscape architect, have a clear understanding of Jellicoe's method, and given their own mutual collaboration the scheme must be rated a considerable success for all concerned. Jellicoe's initial concept is illustrated here, together with the competition submission measured drawings that John and Valerie Winter submitted, remarkably faithful to the original ideas they evolved together.
Michael Spens

The aim is to develop the Bridge area as the historic heart of the town in a way that is attractive and lively for residents and visitors alike. The Bridge is to be made a very special place, and each street around it is to have its own individual character.

St Matthew's is set outside the site, but with the adjacent Garden of Remembrance forms a dramatic starting point for our journey through the centre of Walsall.

High Street is an historic street, and still retains fine old buildings. In the plan it is unchanged except for the rill. The steps at the south-east end are changed for a pool with a tipping water sculpture, which will discharge water at regular intervals. The water flows down the centre of the High Street, cleaning and refreshing, as in many streets in Paris. This rill is so shallow that it in no way impedes movement of cars, but nevertheless crossing places for pedestrians are provided in two positions. The architecture of Market Square is currently out of fashion and is certainly not of a high order, but the buildings appear to have many useful years of life ahead of them and it is proposed to cover most of them with a white metal trellis and to plant ivy, roses and other plants to give a pleasant character appropriate to a market.

Concept sketches by Sir Geoffrey Jellicoe

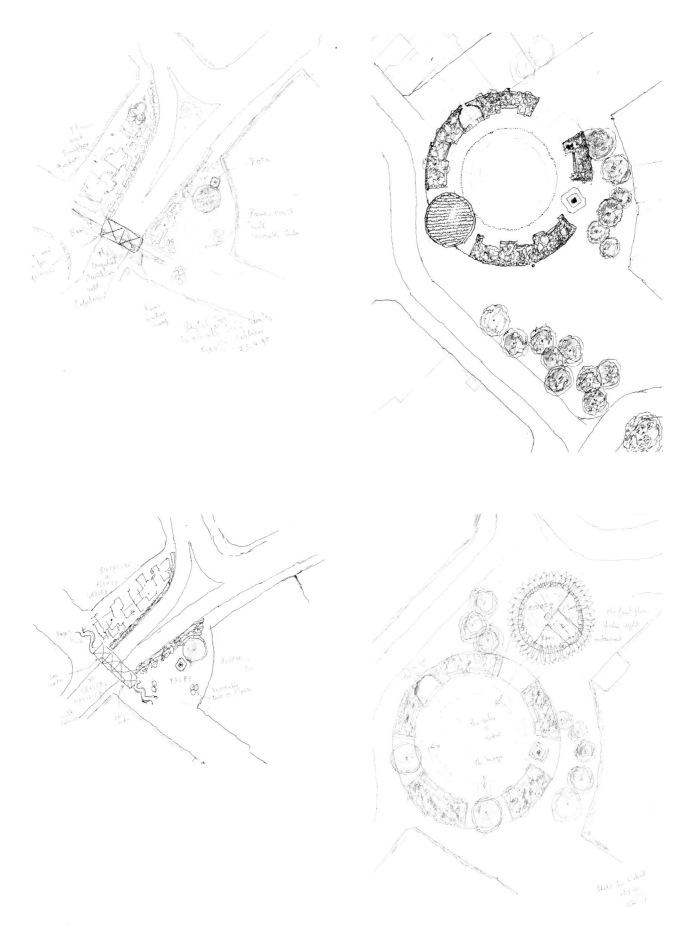

107

A tented roof of fibreglass, coated with Teflon or silicon to give a forty year life, is stretched over Digbeth. This will keep the rain out but let the light in, giving a festive air. Thus this part of the market forms a suitable entrance to the Bridge and creates a covered space for civic events if rain makes the Bridge unsuitable. This is the core of the design which seeks to create a new and ordered urban space without affecting the buildings. It is entered through gates placed in railings, which are only closed on civic occasions, but give a sense of entering a formal, and rather special place. Names of distinguished former citizens are engraved on the railings to give an awareness of continuing history. Inside the railings New York stone paving is laid; there is no decorative patterning, but it is arranged in squares within a grid of granite set gutters which take surface water to drains.

To the north, shielding the town centre from traffic, is the Crystal Pavilion. To the west is a vehicle route marked by bollards and with new trees planted at the St Paul's Road end enclosing a cycle stand. In the centre of the Bridge is a circular area defined by planted areas and two fountains. The outside of this circle is a holly hedge, clipped on the outside and left to grow on the inside and enclosing shrubs and flowers sloping down towards the inside of the circle. The holly hedge is permanent, but some of the planting within – shrubs in containers and bedding plants – can be changed with the seasons. Planting is surrounded by a granite-faced dwarf wall surmounted by a stainless steel mesh forming a relatively dry and clean seat. Recesses in the dwarf wall provide more comfortable seats with backs.

To one side of the seating area is a raised dais, covered in dark granite and used for civic or entertainment occasions. Four thousand people can stand within the circle and here they will hear election results, watch performers or see the Christmas tree. Within the circle black and white stone paving slabs are laid to form a maze, at the centre of which is a round stone, inscribed around its circumference 'This is the centre of Walsall'.

Bradford Street has the same paving and vehicle route marked by bollards as the Bridge. The paving is taken straight across and a line of trees is

OPPOSITE: Aerial view looking north-east

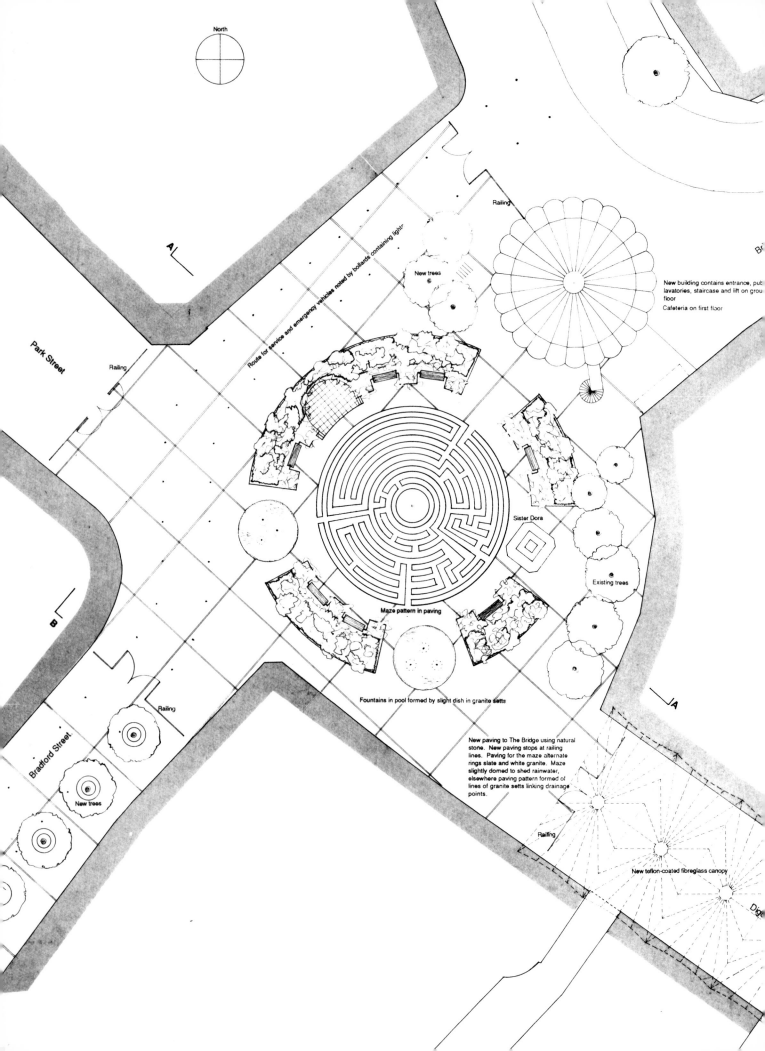

North

Park Street

A

B

Railing

Railing

Route for service and emergency vehicles noted by bollards containing light

New trees

Railing

New building contains entrance, pub
lavatories, staircase and lift on grou
floor
Cafeteria on first floor

Sister Dora

Existing trees

Maze pattern in paving

Fountains in pool formed by slight dish in granite setts

New paving to The Bridge using natural
stone. New paving stops at railing
lines. Paving for the maze alternate
rings slate and white granite. Maze
slightly domed to shed rainwater,
elsewhere paving pattern formed of
lines of granite setts linking drainage
points.

Bradford Street

Railing

New trees

Railing

A

New teflon-coated fibreglass canopy

Dig

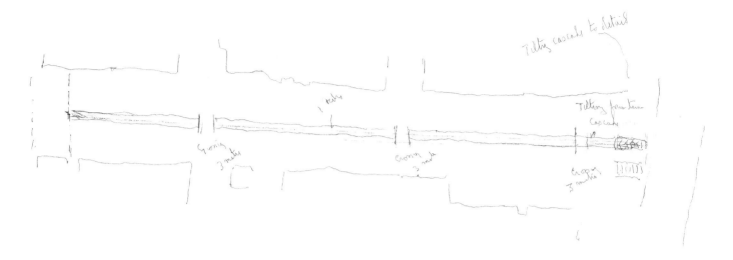

planted down the centre. Around the trees are seats. Park Street remains unchanged, and St Paul's Street can be reconsidered jointly with the designers of the new bus station. Bridge Street is unchanged, except that the traffic route to St Paul's Street is made narrower.

The Crystal Pavilion is optional. If it is not viable financially in the short term, then a circular rose garden, 16 metres in diameter, should be planted. The circular form is important to the design and if the rose garden option is adopted then the circle should be placed exactly in the position indicated by the Pavilion.

The Crystal Pavilion has a solid base. A battered wall, faced with granite, encloses lavatories for men, women and disabled persons, with an entrance, a kitchen and a staircase and lift to the first floor. The upper level includes a restaurant/cafeteria/wine bar and is constructed entirely in glass. Glass walls give access to a balcony all round, lightly constructed with checker plate floor and glass balustrade. Glass columns support roof beams which radiate from the lift shaft in the centre. These roof beams are of glass with

white dots printed on to give sun shading; they support a roof of toughened glass, double glazed over the building, and with projecting curved ends over the balcony. A light spiral staircase connects the balcony with the ground so that, on fine days, the coffee bar can spill over into the surrounding space.

Market stalls will be supplied with water and electricity and the fabric roofs renewed in jolly colours. The stalls will be adapted so that counter boards slide into a vertical position to allow cars to park when the market is closed.

Existing buildings are, with a few exceptions, of dull design and often too low to enclose space in a true urban manner. The competition budget allows little more than a clean-up so the design has been made in such a way that the quality of the buildings is not a key issue. Planning policies should not aim at a cohesive design but should encourage good modern design of buildings at least three or four storeys high. As designers we have strong ideas as to what any new or altered building should look like, but would not wish to make proposals

without knowledge of a building's function and discussions with owners and users.

Lighting is a key element as it is hoped that The Bridge will be civilised and safe after dark. For the main lighting it is hoped to persuade users of surrounding buildings to allow metal halide lights to be placed behind each upper floor window emphasising the silhouette and reversing the daytime pattern of the facades. The Crystal Pavilion will be brilliantly lit internally, spilling light in all directions. Uplighters in Digbeth will throw light on the underside of the tents, illuminating the whole of the area below. Towards the centre of The Bridge, lighting is lower both in height and in intensity, with luminaires in the trees, in the planting beds and in the dwarf walls. Focal lighting is provided for the dais. In Bradford Street, lights are placed in the trees and low level lights below the seats throw light across the paving. *John and Valerie Winter*

OPPOSITE: Site plan; ABOVE: Concept sketch by Sir Geoffrey Jellicoe

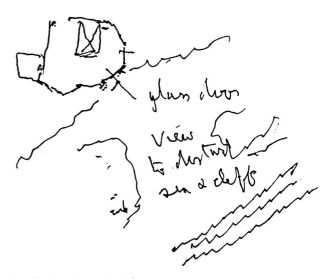

STATEMENT

SIR GEOFFREY JELLICOE
MICHAEL SPENS

To become an art rather than a craft, landscape design must be an amalgamation of the two worlds of Jung, the conscious and the subconscious. As a generality the landscape painter will originate an idea in his subconscious and thereafter search the real world for its expression. The art lies in the visible amalgamation of the abstract with the real.

The landscape designer cannot do this for the origins of his work, ie, the client, site, nature and technique of all kinds, are such to swamp all encouragment of a creative subconscious (except that of a genius, who would probably be incompetent as a practitioner).

So important is it to the profession that landscape design should have the status of an art that I have devised a purely intellectual way of making it so. I impregnate the drawing-board design with an invisible idea apparent only to the subconscious of the visitor.

Since the purpose of art is to uplift the spirit, I place within the drawing an idea of some earthly perfection of shape (human, animal, vegetable, poetry, symphony etc). This subconscious force distorts reality without the visitors' consciousness being aware of it. My first experiment with the soft underbelly of the serpent, Hemel Hempstead Water Gardens, 1954; my last proposed symphony at Atlanta, 1993, where gently it subconsciously takes charge of the conscious, mighty though this may be.

NOTE: Complimentary to all this, of course, is the subconscious beauty of classical geometry. Art from Landscape, *24 February 1995.* Sir Geoffrey Jellicoe

In May 1995 Sir Geoffrey Jellicoe quietly migrated out of London to the Channel coast of the West Country of England. A determined move, this has marked a further stage in a long career. Although the drawing board has been folded away, he remains actively aware of current issues in the field of landscape which he has tended and worked so diligently for over seventy years.

The move to the remote Channel coast is something even more fundamental to Jellicoe's way of thinking. In a letter dated in July 1995, soon after the relocation, Jellicoe

has described a nine-sided space for living, from which habitat he is constantly aware of the changing moods of nature over sea and cliffs. At Rustington, Sussex, Jellicoe spent much of his childhood in the period before 1914. Shore and seas here had a profound influence on him. Now, on the Devon coast, he is back.

There are still visitors, limited by time. Gary Doherty, an Irish landscape student at University College, Dublin has made a comparative study of the work of two masters, Jellicoe and Burle Marx, seen as representing the two extremes of twentieth-century landscape design; Jellicoe as philosopher/architect, Burle Marx as painter/botanist. Doherty obtained a series of interviews with Jellicoe, and the last took place earlier this year after the move. That was one of the first visits to the new place Jellicoe had found. Doherty describes it:

'The ground clearly visible from the nine-sided space is lacking in form and function. Jellicoe does not find this new environment a challenge; life has found a new rhythm at a more suitable pace. The environment we live in certainly has a major influence on life, and the job of the landscape architect of the future is to encompass the landscape as a totality as well as being composed of individual or particular places. Although from two very different backgrounds, Jellicoe and Burle Marx have both reached a similar conclusion, that the role of the landscape architect can only be one of increasing performance in the twenty-first century. Burle Marx once claimed that, "A jewel is to man as man is to nature". We must look at the small things for beauty as well as to the large.'

I had visited Jellicoe there on one stormy and overcast day in mid-October 1995. In the sense defined by the Irish philosopher Burke over two hundred years ago, the Sublime had returned, as the sea beat against the cliffs, and the rains beat against the windows of Jellicoe's new habitat. *Michael Spens*